origins

egypt, west asia and the aegean

To Paul, Ken and Johannes, without whose encouragement this history of architecture would never have been undertaken, and to Tom and Jon, without whose imagination and patience it would never have been published.

● ● ● ellipsis

origins

egypt, west asia and the aegean

First published 1998 by
●●●ellipsis
55 Charlotte Road
London
EC2A 3QT
EMAIL ...@ellipsis.co.uk

ISBN 1 899858 38 5

Publisher Tom Neville
Designed by Jonathan Moberly
Edited by Vicky Wilson
Drawings by John Hewitt
Drawings on pages 72-73 and 119-23 generated by Matthew
Taylor from CAD models by Nick Gadsby and Ian Stewart at
Kent Institute of Art and Design
Image processing by Heike Löwenstein
Glossary by Andrew Wyllie
Index by Diana LeCore
Printed and bound in Hong Kong

British Library Cataloguing in Publication Data: a catalogue
record for this publication is available from the British Library

contents

I **Nomadic tent, modern Iran.**

For most of his life man has been a nomadic hunter and gatherer. In the protracted process of climatic change affecting the distribution of food resources that accompanied the retreat of the last Ice Age, however, people learned to breed plants and animals. Evidence for this first appears in the 8th millennium BC at various sites between the Aegean coast of Anatolia and the Zagros highlands of Iran. Permanent settlement here was a millennium further on, but the regular seasonal abandonment of camps[1] or caves[2] for farming villages with granaries and mills on fertile, well-watered land with good lines of communication established many sites for later towns. And the common forms of tent – circular and conical or rectangular and pitched – were naturally reproduced in timber and pressed mud, plastered reeds or dry stone with thatch.

Early settlements
The earliest signs of settlement have been found in the upper Euphrates and Jordan valleys. The oldest inhabited site is probably Jericho, where they were

2 OVERLEAF **Cappadocia, limestone landscape with caves.**

building with sun-dried bricks early in the 8th millennium BC. It would be hard to overestimate the importance of this innovation for the advance of building technology, though many centuries were to pass before mud loaves were superseded by rectangular blocks.[3] Well before its disruption c. 7000 BC, the settlement was ringed with a wall of undressed stone. This is the earliest-known fortification, but it is hardly likely that Jericho alone had the organisational skill and resources for monumental public works.

The houses at Jericho, as at most primitive sites, were circular at first, but early in the 7th millennium BC – earlier still on the Euphrates – there were court-yards surrounded by rectangular rooms. At the 6th-millennium site of Catal Huyuk in southern Anatolia, each of the timber and mud-brick houses had a similar rectangular living room.[4] As the houses were contiguous in an extended hive-like complex without courts or even lanes, light penetration and access over the flat roofs were through openings in the upper walls (clerestory). While the degree of standardisation asserts centralised authority, the organic approach suggests the extended family of a matrilineal society.

3 **Brickmaker from Bam, modern Iran.**

Some rooms at Jericho, distinguished by a pedestal opposite the door, seem to have been shrines. At Catal Huyuk several rooms are marked as dedicated to a fertility cult by figures identified as the mother goddess and by bulls' heads.[5-6] The bull or ram and the erect stone or tree trunk (later dressed as a pillar) are ubiquitous symbols of male fertility.

Earth mother or sky god

Fundamentally different attitudes were promoted by the contrasting lifestyles of the farmer and the pastoralist. The latter was primarily concerned with appeasing the forces of the sky, manifest most cogently in the life-threatening storm, which was seen as male and often symbolised as a bird of prey. The former, on the other hand, was mesmerised by the mysteries of fertility and growth, the response of the earth to sun and water (the emergence of life from seeds planted in little holes in the first, penetrated by the two last), which he associated with the earth mother. Usually coupled with a vegetation god, who died in the winter of his impotence each year, she ruled through her priestess, whose annual consort was a *fainéant* king. The fading sun was his; hers was the

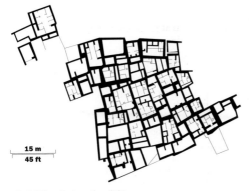

4 **Catul Huyuk** plan of neolithic town.

Note the measure of protection provided to the cellular organism by the unfenestrated external walls.

First occupied in the late 8th millennium and extending over 80 hectares (32 acres), the site seems to have been settled for some 1500 years. The prosperity of the community derived as much from control of nearby quarries of obsidian (coveted for tools) as from agriculture. The inhabitants worked deposits of copper, too, and after nearly 1000 years of hammering it cold had learned how to smelt it before the end of the 7th millennium.

5 **Catal Huyuk, shrine with bulls' heads below one of the earliest-known icons of the mother goddess**
reconstruction (Ankara, National Museum).

    The juxtaposition of the bulls' heads and mother goddess figure has been taken to represent the former issuing from the latter.

6 **Catal Huyuk, mother goddess** (Ankara, National Museum).

The figure is shown giving birth. The heads of the goddess and the animal to her left have been restored, but otherwise this is the world's oldest extant freestanding sculpture.

enigmatic moon, given to phases but constant in brightness, mistress of the waters and the potency of animals.

Faith in the mother goddess, mystical but secure, tended to promote resignation and gratitude, sensuality and emotionalism. Reliance on the terrible and unpredictable sky gods, demanding constant alertness in search for the key to placating them, tended to promote questioning and rationalism. The efficiency of the tribe depended on the physical and mental agility of the men at the head of mobile family units, and the hazards of their existence encouraged polygamy. Primitive agricultural society, on the other hand, luxuriated in the organic growth of extended families from matriarchs, and the need for drones encouraged polyandry. From India to Greece, rich mythologies related the rape or marriage of the agrarians by the pastoralists – particularly the so-called Indo-European Aryans from the steppes of central Asia, who moved south through the Caucasus and west into Europe. In combination or confrontation, they will be of fundamental importance in our history of architecture.

The emergence of civilisation

It is important to remember that civilisation emerged with agriculture, when people realised that life in the wild was not the only way, and that by co-operating with their fellows in settled society they could more easily grow their food on adjacent fields. Developing along with agriculture, villages were most resilient in areas of high rainfall, though special challenges were offered by river valleys such as the Nile or Euphrates,[7-8] where the annual flood brought new soil to replenish exhausted land. It was here, where water-borne transport facilitated communication and trade, that civilisation first arose with the organisation of society under authoritarian rulers in cities. Its development was marked by the ordered deployment of resources, the fostering of special crafts among citizens freed from direct involvement in growing food, the invention of writing, mathematics and time-keeping, and the standardisation of language, beliefs and law.

7 **The Nile valley with Saqqara in the distance.**

8 **The Euphrates valley at Halabiya.**

9 **Karnak, Great Temple of Amun, heb-sed festival hall, relief of Senwosret I** king of Egypt (1971–1926 BC) (Cairo, Egyptian Museum).

3000 BC is often taken as the starting point for the history of civilisation and of architecture in particular – though, of course, to speak of a starting point is misleading when dealing with a slow process of evolution as villages became towns, towns became cities, and cities won kingdoms. Well before then, the tent-like hut was superseded by the house of rectangular rooms, as dry stone or pressed mud (pisé) were superseded by matted and plastered reeds (wattle and daub) or sun-dried brick (adobe), and the shrine was distinguished from the living room. It was about 3000 BC, however, that the state ideal was first embodied in an enduring monumental building – several hundred years after the first empire was won.

The Nile valley, with its numerous settlements protected from the outside world by the desert, became a single entity with the unification of Egypt c. 2900 BC. Mesopotamia, the land of the twin rivers with no natural frontiers, had numerous advanced urban settlements well before this, but they were not forged into an empire until nearly 1000 years later. The cities of the Indus valley emerged about 500 years later still, those of the Aegean and China some 500 years on, and the first American ones 500 years on again. We shall begin with Egypt and West Asia and the Aegean.

The Nile valley

Increasingly attractive to the north-African Hamitic nomads following the desiccation of the Sahara after the last Ice Age, the Nile seems not to have seen settled agriculture until well into the 5th millennium BC – when the idea probably came from Palestine, like writing and building with bricks. Villages replaced tribal camps, some growing into market towns. Clan authority was sustained over these along sections of the river large enough for the organisation of efficient irrigation. These were later to become provinces. Well before written records begin, c. 3200 BC, the clan territories of the delta to the north of modern Cairo and those strung out along the main course of the river nearly to Aswan in the south were welded into states, the kingdoms of Lower and Upper Egypt respectively.

Egyptian cosmology

These kingdoms had many gods descended from primitive animistic and fertility cults, above all those of the earth mother and her seasonal partner, source of fertility, donor of the flood, dying to live again. Each god belonged to a particular locality, and their powers often overlapped. As a locality rose in importance – from village to market town to provincial centre, for instance – so too did its gods. And as one locality eclipsed another their gods were combined – hence the rise of syncretic icons with human bodies and animal heads. Ultimately the coalescence of the two kingdoms superimposed a state pantheon of grouped syncretic deities over the local ones – all tolerant of one another. Thus the main god of Heliopolis, a Lower Egyptian seat of power, achieved supremacy as the sun god Re, and accommodated the creator god Ptah of Memphis, another important Lower Egyptian city, in his pantheon as patron of craftsmen – if still associated with the progenitive bull Apis.

Egyptian cosmology allots the sky to a goddess (Nut) who regularly swallows and gives birth to the sun (in which capacity she is the mother goddess Hathor). In the stable climatic conditions of the Nile valley, with its regular inundations of soil-bearing water but little rain, agriculturalists were impressed by the sky more as the realm of the life-giving sun than of the life-threatening storm. Dependent on water-borne

10 Abydos, granite tomb stele of Horus name of Zet (Wadjit) king of Egypt, I dynasty, c. 2900 BC (Paris, Louvre).

The snake adopted here is presumably the cobra of Wadjit, protective goddess of the north. The king had three types of name: the Horus name establishing divine paternity in Horus; the throne name including the words for king from south and north and asserting divine paternity in Re (later Amun-Re); the birth name preceded by 'son of Re'. From the IV dynasty each of the last two was framed by a cartouche (an oval fillet over a short line representing a knotted rope and symbolising the eternal cycle).

transport, they saw the sun god Re travelling across the sky in a boat and changing boats to travel back through the underworld at night.

Taking the prime role in creation, on emerging from the primordial deep with reed and palm on an island – the sacred mound of Heliopolis – Re produced the progenitors of earth (Seb) and sky (Nut). (The ambiguity here, if not testimony to the sun's relatively late rise to religious pre-eminence, is indicative of the conservative belief in an immutable cyclical order.) Seb and Nut produced Isis and Nephthys (twin goddesses of love, procreativity and protection), Osiris (divine king of life on earth), and Seth (god of evil, including confusion, storms and war). Seth killed and dismembered Osiris to usurp his throne, but Isis found the parts (some say except the genitals), reconstituted him and together they produced the falcon-like Horus (miraculously, for those who believed there were no genitals to penetrate her virginity). Transfigured as a star, Osiris became king of the dead (promising resurrection, as god of the ever-recurring flood and of vegetation which dies in winter but is reborn in spring) and Horus won back his throne. Isis and Osiris (and Seth) acknowledged the paternity of the northern god

Re, while Horus was claimed as ancestor by the kings of the south. Their line was thus divine, and the unity of Egypt descended from it as they triumphed and each of them in turn became Horus, son of Osiris, with whom his predecessor had been re-identified in the eternal cycle.

Pharaonic Egypt

According to a history written for the Ptolemaic rulers c. 280 BC, Upper and Lower Egypt were united 30 dynasties earlier under Menes. At the close of the 4th millennium BC, the achievement was commemorated on a tablet of the southern king Narmer. The unifier established himself under the protection of Horus at the seat of northern power, Memphis: this is represented in the royal title on a stele of one of Narmer's early successors by the image of the falcon god over the gate to the capital emblazoned with the king's own sign.[10] For nearly 3000 years the pharaohs (kings) wore the combined crowns of the two realms[9] and the vulture and cobra of the protective deities of south and north – Nekhbet and Wadjit – as does Tutankhamun (see 11, page 30). All the offices of state were doubled too.

Though there were periods when this unity in duality dissolved under the impact of factionalism or invaders, among the 31 dynasties which ruled over the long and conservative history of pharaonic Egypt there were several with an astonishing succession of able monarchs. Notable among these were the III dynasty and the IV dynasty of the Old Kingdom (c. 2575–2134 BC), which consolidated the realm, the XII dynasty of the Middle Kingdom (c. 2040–1640 BC), which extended it to include Nubia (northern Sudan), and the XVIII and XIX dynasties of the New Kingdom (c. 1550–1070 BC), which took Egyptian rule to Asia.

Memphis remained the capital throughout the Old Kingdom and most later rulers had a palace there. The XI and XVII dynasties, which were responsible for turning the tide against the invaders of the first and second intermediate periods respectively, came from the deep south and established their base, called Thebes by the Greeks, as the national capital. The great pharaohs of the XII dynasty moved back north to a new seat near Memphis. The imperial monarchs of the XVII dynasty took Thebes to its greatest glory, but their successors again favoured Memphis or other delta towns. Like the sites of temples, these seats of power, with their bureaucrats, priests and workers, would have been large settlements, attractive to artisans and traders. But Egyptian society was not bourgeois in the modern sense or as we shall find it in Mesopotamia: most Egyptians lived in villages.

Solar worship was at its height between the III and VI dynasties, when the king was seen as the physical son of Re, the unassailable manifestation of divine order (*ma'at*) on earth, who ultimately joined his father on the solar bark for the eternal recrossing of the heavens. But after the disintegration of the Old Kingdom and foreign invasion, certainty about this diminished. When the south reasserted itself against the usurpers and Thebes eclipsed Memphis, the Theban god Amun – who annexed the fertility god Min, married the war goddess Mut and fathered the moon god Khons – absorbed Re and his role in creation. The royal cult of Re was eclipsed by that of Osiris as the once-living king, descended from heaven and resurrected from the dead to triumph as lord of the afterlife.

The Middle Kingdom pharaoh was the incarnation of Horus, mediator between the gods and man but not quite a god himself until assimilated on his death with his father, Osiris. Responsible for sustaining *ma'at* on

earth, protector of the commonweal, he was careworn
in his portraits rather than sublimely confident as in
the past. In the New Kingdom the king was still the
supreme provider, but as Amun's warrior he was also
the hero with all the physical attributes of the perfect
athlete – like his foreign opponents. In his coffin
and the court of his funerary temple he is represented
as Osiris mummified in full regalia.[11] After triumph
abroad and the example of Amenhotep III
(1391–1353 BC), the pharaoh's pretensions to divinity
in this life as the son of Amun-Re were revived in colossal images (see 56, pages 136–37).

The pharaoh was the chief administrator, the com-
mander of the army and the high priest of all temples.
He ruled through a formidable bureaucracy: indeed,
his astonishing buildings depended on a facility for
organisation, developed with flood control, rather
than technological innovation. Near the end of the Old
Kingdom the grip of the king loosened and the bureaucracy ran under its own momentum. The process
repeated itself late in the Middle and New Kingdoms.

By the end of the XVIII dynasty the pharaoh's
prowess as the warrior of Amun was backed by a
standing army, and in gratitude for its success enor-

mous estates were bestowed on the temples of Amun. Their inflated priesthood – a bureaucracy in itself – rivalled the civil administration. Amenhotep III challenged the priests of Karnak by reasserting the divinity of the living pharaoh as the son of Amun, and celebrated his own divine birth in the building of the Great Temple of Luxor (southern Thebes) (see 54, page 133). His son, as Akhenaton (1353–1333 BC), went much further: he denied Amun and the traditional pantheon and presented himself as intermediary for devotion solely to the sun, the source of all life manifest in its disc (Aton), in a monotheism paralleled only by Judaism. His intolerance alienated almost

11 Inner gold coffin of Tutankhamun king of Egypt (1333–1323 BC) (Cairo, Egyptian Museum).

Identifying with the mummified Osiris, the king is in full royal regalia of collar, bracelets and sceptres – the flail (*nekhekh*) of the north and the crook (*heka*) of the south. On his headdress are the vulture of the Upper Egyptian goddess Nekhbet and the cobra of her Lower Egyptian counterpart, Wadjit. These appear again in cloisonné relief about the king's arms, overlaid on the protective wings of Isis and her sister Nephthys.

everyone, and after his death his young heir, as Tutankhamun, had to disclaim Aton.

The next dynasties, based back in the delta, placed renewed emphasis on Re and Osiris and produced some strong kings – for instance, Ramesses II (1290–1224 BC) and Ramesses III (1194–1163 BC). But for the last millennium of its history, much of Egypt was run by the high priests of Amun – or by foreigners.

As ancient Egyptians were obsessed by the Nile's flood, which destroyed as the precondition of renewal in a continuous cycle, so their religion comprehended the continuum of life after death, prepared for it, and sought to ensure survival through it. In eternal re-enactment of the cosmic cycle and the divine drama of Horus and Osiris, the prime objective of pharaonic civilisation was the preservation of the king's body, which provided a home for his individuality's eternal essence (*ka*, which differed from the 'soul' in being tied to earth). In principle only the pharaoh could join Osiris (in transfiguration as a star), because only the divine had a *ka*. However, as his *ka* needed for eternity all that the king himself had needed on earth, it came to be seen that his servants were necessarily immortal too, and anyone could aspire to join them. But they did not have to accompany him in death. As object and name had equal validity, in lieu of substance, word and image preserved the *ka*. Hence the importance to all Egyptians of the royal tomb and its embellishment.

Mesopotamia: the 'fertile crescent'

The story of Mesopotamia is more complicated – like the capriciousness of its two rivers in contrast with the singular determination of the Nile. There is little evidence of settlement around the Tigris or Euphrates before 6000 BC – and this is in the north, where rainfall is sufficient to support agriculture. In the 6th millennium, however, agriculture was freed from dependence on rainfall through the introduction of irrigation. This was crucial for the settlers of inhospitable Sumer: indeed, it was precisely because life was so precarious in southern Mesopotamia that civilisation first emerged there.

Lacking natural resources, the Sumerians had to excel at trade to meet their needs for stone, timber and metal – for weapons, tools and buildings. They also had to co-operate with each other to master the flood to obtain fertile earth and water. The prerequisite skill at organisation and consequent surplus production, varied land values and wealth, growth and stratification of the population, and commercial and industrial specialisation all promoted the emergence of the first cities. Civilisation begins with these, and primacy among them is claimed by Eridu and Uruk. Before the latter eclipsed the former, c. 4000 BC, standardised bricks were being made in rectangular frames; soon after, pottery was being mass produced to standard forms on a wheel. The wheel was applied to transport before the end of the Uruk period (c. 3200 BC) and it was from Uruk that the first traces of writing were recovered. With writing history begins.

Some 13 city-states had emerged in Sumer by the end of the 4th millennium BC. Beyond the cities and their suburbs were villages, fields and groves. Each city belonged to a particular deity and the dominant building was the temple, the god's earthly residence – though traces of early palaces have been uncovered at Kish (see 31, page 86) and Eridu. At Eridu, among the earliest Sumerian remains, shrines date back to c. 5500 BC. Most of these had only one room, but the temple had developed into a sophisticated complex well before the end of the 4th millennium BC, as at Uruk (see 27, pages 78–79). By then the god's household was extensive, and its head ruled not only by virtue of his status as a high priest but as controller of the economy. Crucial to the life of the urban community, obviously, was the collection and ordered distribution of resources, and this was bound to be controlled by the administrator of the god's estate, who must also have dominated trade.

Enviable prosperity provoked warfare, prompted the development of armies and promoted military leaders. Inter-city rivalry apart, since the irrigated areas which supported the cities were separated by grazing land of variable quality, the settled agriculturalists were in constant contact and potential conflict with the nomadic hunting or herding tribes drawn from the periphery of Arabia or the mountains of Iran. At the dawn of history in the late 4th millennium BC, the cause of trouble serious enough to warrant a shift in the structure of power in Sumer seems likely to have been the forceful intrusion of the Semites, a race of nomads from Arabia.

The power of the military leader inevitably grew and the Sumerians ultimately acknowledged a tradition of supreme kingship. Their ancient 'King List' accords supremacy to Eridu before recording the Great Flood, then to Kish. For two centuries from c. 2600 BC supremacy is not credited to any one city for long, though Ur, Uruk and Lagash are prominent and each may have led some form of confederation before succumbing to Umma. By 2350 they were all in the grip of the Semites under Sargon the Great of Akkad. Extroverted ambition took the Akkadians from the Gulf to the Mediterranean, before they over-reached themselves – but they established the model for the warrior king and the military super-state,[12] to be emulated by many. Meanwhile, the city-states reasserted themselves. Ur, chief beneficiary of the expansion of sea trade in the Akkadian era, won hegemony and ruled through the world's first bureaucracy until destroyed by Elam (south-western Iran) c. 2000. New Semitic infiltrators, the Amorites, filled the void.

12 **Susa, stele representing the victory of Naramsin over the Elamites** c. 2250 BC (Paris, Louvre).

Naramsin, the grandson and successor of Sargon the Great, took Akkadian power to its apogee.

Sumerian cosmology

The patron deity with which each Sumerian city had
emerged from its agrarian antecedents was recognised
by the other city-states. Varied fortune led to assimilation – especially after the Semites shook complacent
parochialism – and promoted a handful of gods to general significance. It is impossible now to identify a
primitive Sumerian religion among the fertility cults
common to prehistoric farmers, but by historical times
the intercourse of natives and nomads had fathered a
composite culture. Its cosmology clearly demonstrates
this: the primordial ocean (the goddess Nammu) gave
birth to the female earth and male sky, who in turn produced the gods of sweet water and air, Enki and Enlil.
Enlil, separating his parents and relegating his father
(Sumerian An, Semitic Anum) to outer space, established earth's atmosphere, where he unleashed wind
and storm (Semitic Adad) but regulated the course of
the sun (Sumerian Utu, Semitic Shamash) and moon
(Nanna or Sin) to dispel darkness and set life in
motion. He was recognised as the divine king. The
domain of the earth mother, impregnated by Enki but
impervious to the clarity of Enlil's empyrean, remained
one of dark mystery cohabited by Ninhursag, goddess

of fertility, Ereshkigal, goddess of death, and Inanna (Semitic Ishtar), goddess of love and war. There were many other deities representing facets of being, all with consorts and all conceived in idealised human form.

Kingship

Sovereignty belonged to the gods, and man was made to serve them. Enlil sent kingship down to Sumer as the instrument of heaven: the king's obedience to the gods, the fount of justice, was rewarded by their favourable disposition manifest in adequate flood, and he was reconsecrated at each spring festival when fertility was reinvoked with the deity's remarriage. In accordance with a Semitic ideal, the king was also the supreme warrior and divine favour was obvious in his success at expanding the territory of his flock (see 16, pages 48–49). In Lagash resurgent after the Akkadians, on the other hand, the Sumerian ideal ruler reappears as the pious Gudea, architect of the temple.[13]

After 2000 BC the tent-dwelling Amorites subjected the fertile crescent to their rule in several kingdoms, from which Babylon, Assyria and Mari had emerged predominant by c. 1800 BC. Their capitals were dominated by the palaces of their monarchs:

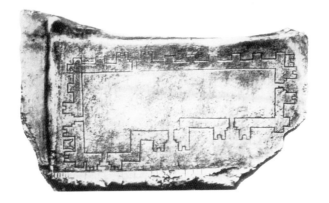

13 **Juxtaposed diorite head and seated figure of Gudea**
ruler (*ensi*) of Lagash, c. 2120 BC (Paris, Louvre).

On his lap is the plan of a walled enclosure (ABOVE).
On his skirt and seat is an inscribed dedication to the
goddess Ningirsu, patron deity of Lagash, and a description
of the construction of the temple of the goddess, which is
known from other surviving texts to have been the major
element in an extensive walled complex.

Hammurabi, who established the ideal of southern unity in Babylon where the two rivers were closest; Shamshi-Adad I, who controlled the north from Ashur on the Tigris; and Zimrilim, whose power at Mari rested on control of the central reach of the Euphrates and the routes west to the Mediterranean, where the Phoenicians ran a trading empire from such city-states as Byblos and Ugarit. Babylon eliminated Mari and reduced Assyria to vassalage at the apogee of its power under Hammurabi – whose great code of laws asserts that Enlil had ceded to Babylon's god Marduk (Enki's son, also called Bel or Baal: 'the Lord'). The law-giver won such prestige for Marduk that the cultural pre-eminence of Babylon was recognised throughout Mesopotamian antiquity.

The Hittites

The Hittites emerged from the horse-borne Aryan tribes who had entered Anatolia (from the Caucasus or over the Hellespont) by the end of the 3rd millennium BC, sending others such as the Hyksos on to upset Egypt. Winning dominance in a long contest for Asia Minor under the eagle banner of their great sky god,[14] they settled in the domain of Hatti in central Anatolia and contributed to the exhaustion of the Egyptian New Kingdom before falling to the enigmatic 'Sea-Peoples' at the end of the 13th century BC. The city of Ugarit (Ras Shamra), their vassal, shared their fate. Hamash, Cinjirli, Carchemish and other cities of northern Syria, heirs of the Hittites, held independent sway in a power vacuum for several centuries.

The Hittites were one of a number of peoples occupying Asia Minor in the 2nd millennium BC who spoke related languages of the Indo-European group. As these, in turn, are related to a language spoken in 3rd-millennium BC Greece, a west–east movement of Aryans seems most probable. On arrival in Hatti, the Aryans are usually thought to have encountered a non-Indo-European-speaking people who may themselves have followed Assyrian trading colonists from the east – but the origins and position of the Hattians in Anatolian history are obscure. Hurrian influence, also from the near east, seems to have been important in the land of Hatti – the Hurrians may have provided the Hittites with their royal family and certainly provided Hittite kings with queens. As usual with Aryan invaders, the Hittites developed a syncretic pantheon from their own sources, the Anatolian inheritance of

44

14 Hittite king embraced by the sky god Sharruma

rock carving in the Yasilikaya shrine near the remains of
the Hittite capital of Hattusas (Bogazkoy), central Anatolia.

The king is presumed to be the last great Hittite king,
Tudhaliyas IV (c. 1250–1220 BC), who is known to have
reigned under the patronage of Sharruma, son of the great
storm god Teshub and sun goddess Hebat. Gods wear
horned helmets.

The first great Hittite king was Hattusilis I (advent
c. 1650 BC) who extended his sway from Hatti over his
western neighbours and south-east into northern Syria.
The empire reached its peak under Suppiluliumas I
(c. 1380–1334 BC), who absorbed much of Syria, destroyed
the northern-Mesopotamian kingdom of Mitanni and
married the king of Babylon's daughter. His grandson (?)
Muwatallis (c. 1308–1285 BC) had the better of the
encounter with Ramesses II of Egypt at Qadesh, c. 1286,
but dynastic rivalry soon began to weaken the kingdom
of Hatti in the face of aggressive neighbours and the 'Sea-
Peoples'. Fifty years after the death of Tudhaliyas IV, the
empire had disappeared.

15 Kalhu (Nimrud), relief from the throne room of the palace showing Ashurnasirpal II king of Assyria (883–859 BC) (London, British Museum).

The relief shows the king (in the fez-like hat with top-knot reserved for royalty) as high priest of Ashur. Responsible for ensuring the continued bounty of nature in the fertility of the land, he worships Ashur in the winged disc of divinity on either side of a stylised tree. He is supported by winged genii (in the horned cap of divinity, not unlike the Hittite gods), who carry a pail of holy water and some sort of sprinkler. The tree recalls the stylised palm motif (palmette) of Egypt.

the Hattians and the legacy of the Hurrians. They doubtless brought a sky god with them to the kingdom of Hatti and seem to have assimilated him with a local water god, consort of a goddess of the nether-region who probably produced the sun. Then known as the weather god of Hatti and the sun goddess of Arinna, these, in turn, were identified with the Hurrian storm god Teshub and sun goddess Hebat – the former still subordinate to his wife – who produced the great sky god Sharruma.

The Assyrians and their conquerors

The domain of Urartu in eastern Anatolia filled the vacuum left by the Hittites from the early 9th century BC. Then, after several false starts, revived Assyria began its rise. Forging a world empire in which vassal kings were replaced by Assyrian viceroys, its exceptional line of kings reached the apogee of its power

16 OVERLEAF **Kuyunjik (Nineveh), relief from the royal palace showing Ashurbanipal** king of Assyria (669–626 BC) (London, British Museum).

The king is represented hunting lions: responsible for protecting his flock, he is the embodiment of heroism.

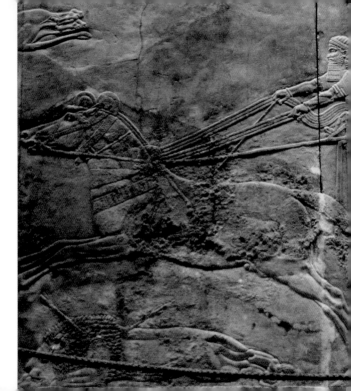

with the conquest of Egypt in 671 BC. Ashurnasirpal II (883–859 BC),[15] who provided the initial impetus, moved from Ashur to a more central base in a grand new palace at Kalhu (Nimrud) – though the old capital remained the cult centre of the supreme god Ashur. Sargon II (722–705 BC), who defeated Urartu and launched the last push through Palestine, moved to an even more splendid seat at Dur-sarrukin (Khorsabad) (see 66, pages 158–59); his son Sennacherib, who sacked Babylon, surpassed even this at Kuyunjik (Nineveh). In the embellishment of these palaces the king is shown as high priest of Ashur, but most memorably as the heroic protector of his flock – as in the relief of Ashurbanipal hunting lions in the type of chariot (light and fast but strong) that had taken so many of his forebears to victory in war.[16]

The last of the great Assyrians, Ashurbanipal (669–626 BC) took the ruthlessness of his predecessors to a new extreme in the conquest of Elam. Overextended and universally hated, his line was eradicated in 612 by resurgent Babylon and the Aryan Medes, recently settled to the north of Elam. The Medes took Urartu and north-eastern Mesopotamia from the Assyrians. The Babylonians reclaimed the south.

After Nebuchadnezzar II (605–562 BC), who asserted his rule over the Levant and made Babylon the greatest city in the world, the neo-Babylonians did not last much longer than 20 years before falling to a new power from Iran. This was Cyrus the Great, who seems to have risen to prominence in embittered Elam and imposed his will over the Medes and their Aryan cousins the Persians, then still in the process of settlement further east. Before he won Mesopotamia, and the immense prestige which went with the title 'King of Babylon', Cyrus' conquest of King Croesus of Lydia took him to the Aegean. Afterwards his Achaemenid line went on to weld most of the world known to them into an empire run at first from his camp at Pasargadae (see 93, page 217). Theirs was a new order (see volume 3, IMPERIAL FORM).

The Jews

Meanwhile a new order of a different kind – of even greater significance for the future – had been established by one of the smaller nations which rose to prominence in the power vacuum left by the elimination of the Hittites. The Jewish chronicles, later enshrined in the Bible, locate the tribes which ultimately constituted the nation of Israel in Chaldea. Early in the 2nd millennium BC, the great patriarch Abraham led them from Ur towards Canaan, the hilly land of Palestine beyond the river Jordan, which they eventually infiltrated. The unfertile land ensured the survival of their pastoralism there, and sent some looking for better conditions elsewhere, notably in Lower Egypt.

The Israelites who settled in Egypt prospered in the century of Egyptian impotence that followed the fall of the Middle Kingdom to the Hyksos, but were reputedly enslaved under the resurgent New Kingdom. Their exodus, led by Moses, is not implausibly dated to the reign of Akhenaton (1353–1333 BC), whose monotheism may not be coincidental with the cataclysmic revelation of Jehovah (Yahweh) to Moses on Mount Sinai. Be that as it may, the Israelite leader and his One True God entered into a covenant: worshipping him only, his chosen people would obey his commandments and he would protect them.

Jehovah was a personal god who intervened in history. Transcendent, he could not be represented. Thus unlike other Mesopotamian deities, cast in the image of man or woman, he had no sensual needs, no consort, no progeny: he was immaculate, and man was unclean. His cult was not dedicated to re-enacting creation myths or fertility rites but to purification and expiation, to commemorating a history of salvation and to sustaining the covenant of the law, the ineluctable moral basis for the religious and social order which set the 'chosen people' apart forever.

Canaan was regained by the followers of Moses after protracted dispute. The nation was constituted as a federation of 12 tribes, but the tribe of Judah – the largest, further enlarged by the absorption of the remnants of depleted tribes – was always distinct from the rest. Kinship through descent from related ancestors (the sons of Abraham's grandson Jacob) was a powerful bond, but above all the tribes acknowledged common faith in Jehovah, whose presence in their midst was symbolised by the Ark of the Covenant which enshrined the tablets on which Jehovah had given his commandments to Moses, and hence common law.

At first disputes among the Children of Israel were settled by judges chosen by God, but the tribes had no real political cohesion, let alone organised government. In the struggle for Canaan, their moral integrity sometimes failed them. They appropriated the sanctuaries of Canaan – usually 'High Places', as in Mesopotamia – for Jehovah, but the old associations persisted and at times inspired syncretism, contrary to the covenant. The consequences of breaking the covenant, the major theme of the biblical Old Testament, were articulated by prophets – teachers and communicators as well as tellers of the future – directly inspired by God: men of the word.

To counter syncretism, the prophets promoted the centralisation of the cult. Towards the end of the 1st millennium BC, kingship was instituted to further the process of political unity among the tribes. Success was limited to the generations of David and Solomon (c. 1010–930 BC). It was they who conceived and realised the cult centre at their new-found seat, Jerusalem in Judah, to enshrine the nation's unique bond, its covenant with the One True God. Intricately if ambiguously described in the Bible, little tangible substance of the Great Temple remains beyond the platform providing its High Place.

After Solomon, Judah was divided from Israel as a separate kingdom. Israel, a vassal of Assyria at various times, was occupied from 732 BC. Towards the end of the following decade, the king of Israel tried to persuade the king of Judah to join a defensive alliance against Assyria and attacked him when he declined. Judah called for Assyrian assistance and remained a protectorate for the rest of Assyrian history. Israel was annihilated by the Assyrians after the final suppression of revolt in the capital, Samaria, in 721 BC. Deprived of protection when Assyria was overcome by the neo-Babylonians and their allies, Judah fell to Nebuchadnezzar II in 587 and the Great Temple was destroyed.

Part successively of the neo-Babylonian, Persian, Seleucid and Roman empires, the Jews had no political state but sustained a religious community, a theocracy based on religious law administered by priests from the rebuilt Great Temple. God was king, as always – the kings had been his viceroys. The ideal king, promoting the kingdom of God on earth, was foreshadowed by David but realised by none of his successors. Sacral psalms prophesying the universal dominion of Jehovah looked for salvation from foreign domination to an individual chosen by God from David's descendants: a second David – the Messiah.

No one area of the world may claim primacy in the invention of architecture. From the western point of view, however, its fundamental principles are clearly established in the traditions of ancient Egypt and Mesopotamia. The differing climatic, geological and topographical conditions of these two areas gave predominance in each to one of the two basic building materials: mud brick (in Mesopotamia) and timber or reeds (in Egypt). These, in turn, dictated the basic structural systems: wall and arch (arcuated)[17] and post and beam (trabeated) (see 20, page 65). These approaches to structure in turn dictated the basic approaches to design, to the conception of the ordering of space: the informal or organic as in the Mesopotamian house and palace, and the formal or rational, with symmetry about a central axis, as in the Egyptian temple. These two seminal traditions also introduce us to the significance of form: pragmatic on the one hand, symbolic or representational on the other – that is, following from the practical requirements of function, structure and situation or going beyond these to convey some

17 **Mari, brick tombs with corbelled arches** early 2nd millennium BC.

special idea. Finally, they demonstrate the operation of patronage and ideology – the way a patron's idea of his or her role in the established order informs the meaning of a building.

Materials and structure

The land of the Tigris and Euphrates seems to have been treeless well before history. The erratic flood was generally not constrained by cliffs that would have limited the extent of inundation and maximised its impact. Thus the main impression is not of a rich green strip but of mud which bakes hard in the sun. From these conditions came the most elemental of building materials: mud or clay, impacted with straw or dung for binding, and sun dried to form bricks which, piled one upon the other, form walls. It was soon seen that these needed protection from the weather. Baking in a kiln was developed for durability – not always for all the bricks needed for a vast walled complex, but at least for an outer skin of glazed ones in lieu of stone. And a malleable material like clay invites moulding or the incision of a pattern – inevitably, in agrarian communities, a free-ranging, fantastic, even symbolic elaboration of motifs drawn from nature. Hence the revetment, sometimes glazed, would be not only protective but also decorative and often didactic.[18]

In the Nile valley, on the other hand, the narrow floodplain, bordered not far from the river by sandstone cliffs, produced plenty of reeds which could be

18 OVERLEAF **Babylon, Ishtar Gate** reconstructed façade (Berlin, Museum of the Near East).

This was the north gate of Babylon, rebuilt under Nebuchadnezzar II after the destruction of the city by the Assyrians in 689 BC. Next to the palace, it guarded the opening of the main axis of the town (see 65, page 156). The name derives from the nearby Temple of Ishtar, the goddess of love and war. The yellow bulls and white dragons, in low relief on the blue-glazed ground, are sacred to Ishtar and the Babylonian deity Marduk respectively.

The circular flower (rosette) in the gate's dado is ubiquitous. In the matching tiled panel from the throne room of Nebuchadnezzar, displayed to the right of the gate, the lotus motif with curved petals superimposed on stems in the centre and the stylised palm-frond motif (palmette) in the border variously relate to the Assyrian sacred tree (see 15, page 46) and the characteristic Egyptian lotus (see 19, page 62).

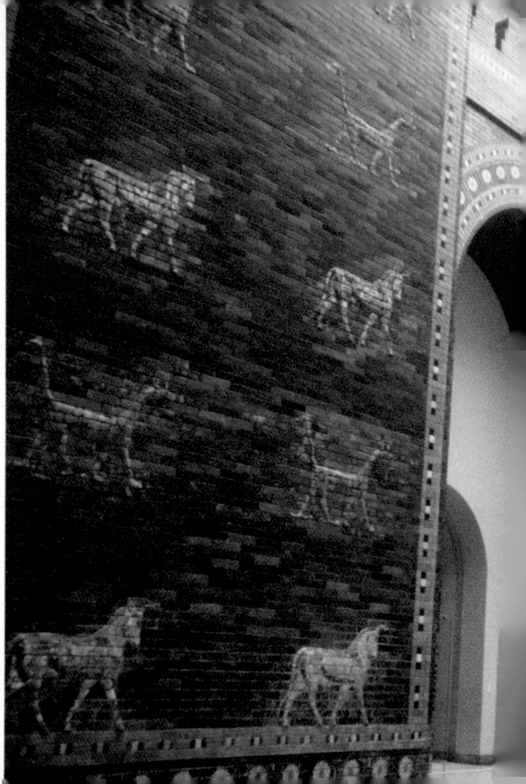

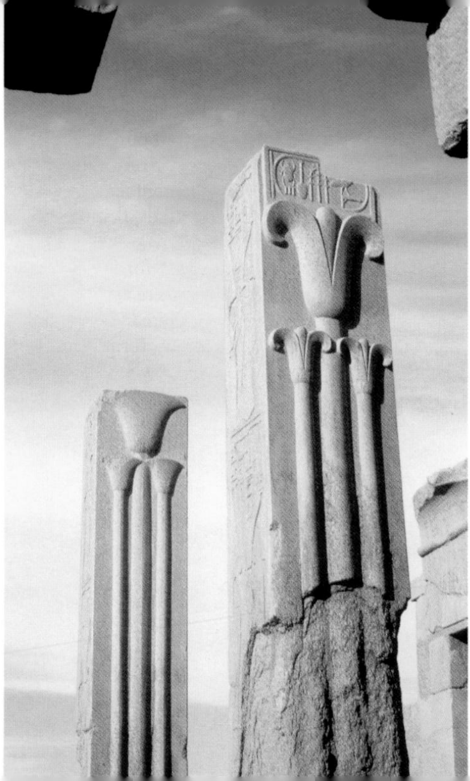

bound together to form posts[19] or woven into screens. It also supported groves of palms, producing soft wood and fronds, easily worked or bound together for use in light structures. The palm or reed bundle were alternative models: in each, the contact of load and support was celebrated with a frond-, flower- or bud-shaped capital.[20]

Groves of trees were cultivated for the food they gave and, as a source of bounty, were associated with the temple: they were seen as sacred. They were as important for the inspiration of form as for the provision of materials: in form as well as substance, as the tree became the column so the grove became the hall. The temple is the island of the creator, and if the plants of the Nile mud flats are recalled in its structure, in the sacred grove is to be found the origin of its hall of many columns. Hardwood, imported by sea from Lebanon in particular, had supplanted the inadequate local product in major buildings by the IV

19 **Karnak, Great Temple of Amun** pillars in the hall of annals of Tuthmosis III (1479–1425 BC).

The stylised lotus and papyrus represent Upper and Lower Egypt respectively.

dynasty, and masonry had been introduced by the end of the 4th millennium BC. Of course, the Egyptians had plenty of mud for bricks too, and – unlike lower Mesopotamians – plenty of stone to complement it in constructing walls and entrance pylons to protect their sacred groves.

Obviously columns present no impediment to the flow of space, but walls must be breached. Masonry is durable under compression, vulnerable in tension. An opening in a wall may be corbelled: the masonry is laid in horizontal courses, each projecting beyond the one below from a certain level until they bridge the gap (see 17, page 56). However, the soundest way of supporting the masonry above a hole in a wall is to bridge it with a semi-circle of bricks (or stones) in the shape of a fan:

20 **Edfu, Temple of Horus** c. 250–116 BC, detail of columns and beams in the hypostyle hall at the head of the inner court.

In this typical Egyptian cult temple, the six columns of the hall façade, screened to half height, and the 12 larger interior columns have a variety of capitals ranging from the traditional palm-frond bundle (background) to variations on the lotus theme (foreground).

the voussoir arch (see 18, pages 60–61). The weight bearing down from above wedges voussoirs tightly together, reinforcing the strength of the bridge. With a flat lintel, obviously, the opposite is true: it is weaker in the centre and must be massive to endure.[21]

Ornamentation and design

In both Mesopotamia and Egypt the properties of the local materials also dictated the approach to embellishment. And the differences between the two dictated that these approaches would be radically disparate. Disposing ornament to elucidate structure (as in the capitals of columns), the Egyptian approach was essentially architectonic. The Mesopotamian approach – for instance masking the wall with free-ranging fantasy in brick or tilework – was just as essentially non-architectonic: compare the Ishtar Gate at Babylon (see 18, pages 60–61) with the hypostyle hall of the Temple of Horus at Edfu (see 20, page 65).

Just as the two areas' basic approaches to structure

21 **Edfu, Temple of Horus** view along the main axis from the hypostyle hall, through the forecourt to the entrance between the twin pylons.

and ornamentation originated in the materials to
hand, so did their basic approaches to design: comprehensively ordered on the one hand (Egypt), basi-
cally organic on the other (Mesopotamia). In a sacred
grove, the planting is likely to have been regular: people have usually been disposed to apparent order in the
belief that the gods of creation are ordering agents –
and so too in building, especially religious building.
And appearances apart, a random set of posts is not
practical: they must bear their load evenly and define
clear axes.[22] On the other hand, there is no incentive
to align spaces when they are screened from one
another by walls.

22 PREVIOUS PAGES **Philae, Temple of Isis** begun mid 3rd
century BC.

A contracted example of an Egyptian processional cult
temple. To the left of the outer court (oblique to the axis
of the temple) is the later 'birth house' (Mammisi Temple,
dedicated to the birth of the pharaoh from Horus and a
mortal mother under the auspices of Isis/Hathor). Beyond
the main entrance pylons, the other elements include an
inner court, hypostyle hall, vestibule and sanctuary.

As we have seen, Sumerian civilisation evolved in an arid plain. Beyond the plain, way off in the distance, were the mountains from which came the bounty of rain but also the havoc of storms. The forces of good and evil – and so the dwelling place of the gods – were therefore associated with high ground, and in his attempt to placate those forces man found it prudent to build mountains for the gods within the orbit of the town.

The ziggurat

Hence the ziggurat – the most monumental of all Mesopotamian building types and as symbolic in its form as the Egyptian hypostyle hall. Clearly there is symbolic purpose in the evolution of the form as a series of terraces, elevating the priest to a point where he could communicate with the all-high. The great Ziggurat of Nanna at Ur is the supreme example.[23] The structure enclosed no space, though there was a domed vestibule – the prototype of the ciborium – and a temple on top. Note, too, how regular is the structure of god compared with that of man cowering beneath it: the block of houses opening on to courts and presenting blind outer walls to narrow lanes.[24–25]

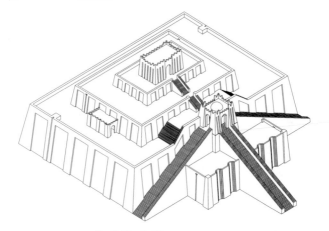

23   **Ur, Ziggurat of Nanna** c. 2100 BC, reconstruction as
built by Urnammu and plan of complex at ground level.

In a compound surrounded by cells and preceded by an
entrance court, the massive artificial mountain – 62 by
43 metres (203 by 141 feet) at its base, about 21 metres
(69 feet) high – rose probably in three stages to the shrine
of Ur's patron deity, the moon god Nanna. It was built of

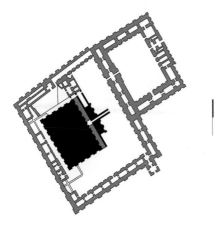

mud brick interleaved with matting for binding, and its
battered and buttressed sides were protected from erosion
by a skin of burned bricks. Three flights of stairs led to
the domed vestibule before the first terrace, two parallel
to the south-east side of the structure, the central one
perpendicular to it. The other two terraces were served by
single flights of stairs continuing the line of the central one.

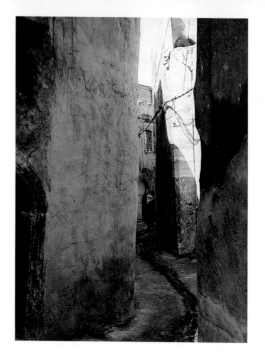

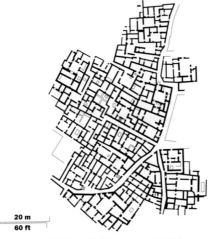

20 m
60 ft

25 **Ur, residential district to the south-east of the citadel** plan.

The citadel was a roughly rectangular enclosure. The settlement to its south developed organically, with the block of houses presenting blind outer walls to narrow lanes.

24 **Mosul (northern Iraq), organic urban development.**

The temple

Though the temple on the summit of the Ziggurat of
Nanna at Ur is lost, the plan of what is thought to be
a temple to the goddess Ningirsu on the lap of Gudea
of Lagash – dating from c. 2120 BC and possibly the
earliest surviving architectural drawing in the world
(see 13, page 41) – conforms in general to a long, conservative tradition.

The earliest Sumerian remains at Eridu (c. 5500 BC)
include a sequence of square cells distinguished from
houses by a recess with a pedestal. A more complex
formula was evolved in the course of the 4th millennium BC: a tripartite block in which the main space
was elongated and flanked by smaller rooms, one of
which contained a staircase to the roof, the other the
entrance – though there was sometimes a door opposite the altar as well.[26] Eridu apart, this first appears
at the northern Mesopotamian site of Tepe Gawra,
where several relatively formal buildings had a dais at
one end of the main space and an altar towards the
centre. The walls were built of standardised bricks and
relieved with buttresses disposed in a regular rhythm
like the reed columns of the people who live in the delta
marshes – evidently then as now.

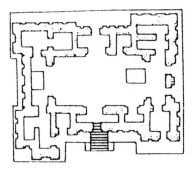

26 **Eridu, temple from level VII** late 5th millennium BC, plan.

This is one of the earliest examples so far recovered of the standard Mesopotamian tripartite arrangement of the nave between ranges of rooms including a staircase to the roof. Entry was from the end opposite the sanctuary and from the sides. The rhythm of the projecting buttresses, perhaps recalling reed-bundle construction, was also to be typical. The practice of rebuilding temples on the same site naturally produced the elevation over the rest of the town that was later to be contrived for the ziggurat.

27 Uruk (Warka) 'White Temple' mid 4th millennium BC,
plan and axonometric.

At a site dedicated to the worship of the sky god Anu,
this 'high' temple, aspiring to the realm of the deity, is
raised some 13 metres (43 feet) above ground on a battered
platform incorporating the impacted remains of earlier

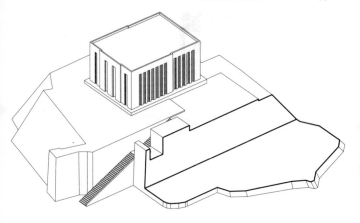

buildings and their platforms. Access was gained by an
elongated staircase to a subsidiary terrace to the north.
The tradition of the tripartite plan is sustained in the shrine
itself, but entry is from either end of the nave as well as from
the side opposite the altar. The name derives from remnants
of whitewash on the buttressed external brickwork.

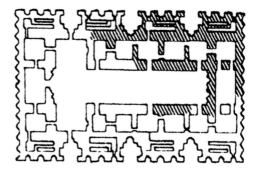

28 Uruk, temple from level IVa late 4th millennium BC, plan.

At the lower Eanna site, dedicated to the worship of the great earth mother and her agents, above all Innana, a transept has been added to the nave before the sanctuary and entry is from each side arm. Built on a cleared and levelled site, this temple seems to represent a category purposely built low, as one might expect in the context of the worship of the earth mother.

Raised on a high terrace as in the so-called 'White Temple' of Uruk dedicated to the worship of the sky god Anu,[27] or on a platform at the head of an elevated enclosure as in the 'Oval Temple' of Khafaje[29] and the main sanctuary of Ishtar in the triple temple at Ischali,[30] the tripartite block was to be the principal element in religious complexes for much of the history of ancient Mesopotamia – with the entrance usually in the end wall opposite the sanctum. The height of the temple's base is not simply to be explained by protection from flood or constant rebuilding on the same site, as the temple was sometimes built on levelled ground. Indeed, many sacred complexes had both a 'high' and a 'low' temple dedicated to sky and earth deities respectively, the latter at the base of the former and built on a minor plinth to give it dignity. This is first known at Uruk, where the lower site of Eanna[28] supplemented the high site of Anu. An early phase of building at Eanna, roughly contemporary with the 'White Temple', incorporated massive columns – most unusually for Mesopotamia. These and all other exposed surfaces were inset with small cones of red, white and black clay, their circular bases forming regular patterns.

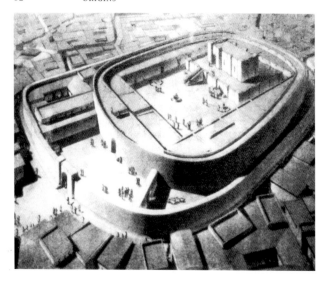

29 **Khafaje, 'Oval Temple'** second half of 3rd millennium BC, reconstructed view.

Within a roughly oval raised compound, similarly curved walls framed a rectangular court higher again than the preceding level and dominated by the shrine on its terrace. Access from compound to court and shrine involved double turns. The temple officials were accommodated in a courtyard complex to the left of the outer court. Magazines for storing the produce offered to the deity filled the space between the curved and rectangular walls of the second court. Towards the centre was an ablution tank and before the temple platform was a sacrificial altar. The corners of the shrine were oriented to the cardinal directions. The whole site was excavated down to virgin soil and the foundations embedded in pure sand from the desert.

30 **Ischali, temple dedicated to aspects of the great
goddess with Ishtar predominant** early 2nd millennium
BC, reconstructed view.

The complex of three temples was raised on the
conventional platform, its corners oriented to the cardinal
directions. The main twin-towered entrance led through
magazines to the southern corner of the generous court
which served two of the three sanctuaries – the third had its
own entrance towards the eastern corner of the complex.
The dominant axis (south-east/north-west) extended up
a flight of steps through another twin-towered gate to the
main sanctuary of Ishtar on the highest level. This too
had its own entrance from the street, at right angles to
the entrance from the first court near the western corner.
Though this was opposite the shrine of the goddess in the
northern corner, access through the main court involved
several turns, as at Khafaje.

30 m
90 ft

31 **Kish, 'Palace A'** first half of 3rd millennium BC, plan.

The remains at Kish are among the earliest of an important Mesopotamian secular building. Descended from the most common form of prehistoric house in the region but rejecting primitive informality, the arrangement of rooms is generally symmetrical within a monumental rectangular enclosure. The nuclear court (1), which presumably provided the main area of asssembly, is assertively square. Even the detached fragment to the south (2), perhaps the royal family's accommodation, is regularly planned.

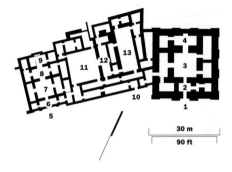

32 **Eshnunna (Tell Asmar), Palace and Temple of Gimilsin** beginning of 2nd millennium BC, plan.

The remains at Eshnunna include a rigorously formal temple with entrance, vestibule, square central court and sanctuary (1–4) aligned on axis in a square enclosure; a similar axial arrangement of the principal elements of the palatine chapel (5–9); and the axial alignment of the square palace court with the throne room (11–12). In accordance with a basic principle of defence, entrance to the palace (10) involves several right-angle turns through an extended series of narrow halls, and procedure beyond the throne room to the inner zone of restricted audience (13) is also off axis.

The palace

By the end of the 3rd millennium BC palaces had
joined temples to dominate the towns of Sumer.[31] An
early example has been uncovered at Tell Asmar (Eshnunna)[32] and a much more extensive and slightly later
one at Mari.[33] As we have noted and this last demonstrates, it is futile to impose a formal order on the plan
of a walled complex because all that may usually be

33   **Mari, Palace of Zimrilim** early 2nd millennium, plan.

Mari's vast palace of about 300 rooms was entered from
the north (1) through three guard rooms, the central one
irregularly shaped and the doors offset from one another to
force the approach through three turns. The main court of
audience (2) was also irregular and addressed from an off-
centre recess for the king (3) which anticipates the *iwan* of
the later Mesopotamian palace tradition. Doors in the four
corners led indirectly to the more private parts of the palace,
that to the south-west to a vestibule (4) between a court
of restricted assembly (5) and the throne room (6). These
regular spaces were aligned on a north–south axis. Beyond
the ceremonial core, the private apartments and service
quarters were knit together by a warren of corridors, and
suggest organic growth.

30 m
90 ft

34 **Mari, Palace of Zimrilim** view from the inner court
to the vestibule before the throne room showing the axial
alignment of the major representational spaces.

appreciated in it is the form of each individual space and the transition to its neighbour. Within the warren of enclosed cells, certainly, regular courts of assembly are aligned with public and private audience rooms.[34] We often find palaces divided into three zones: a formal one for public reception, a semi-formal one for the king himself, and an informal one for the royal women. But if order goes further than the eye can see, it is as though the recently nomadic Semites had imposed some discipline on the prolix organicism of the natives.

35 Saqqara, mortuary complex of Djoser early III dynasty.

The step pyramid lies beyond the heb-sed court. A chapel in the northern style is in the foreground with southern-style chapels centre and right. The heb-sed festival, or royal regeneration ceremony, was usually celebrated in the king's thirtieth year.

As high temples were rising in Mesopotamia to lift man to the plane of the gods, the Egyptians were evolving the step pyramid as a tomb to accommodate the god-king for eternity. The greatest example was built c. 2700 BC for the III-dynasty king Djoser at Saqqara.[35-36] As we know, the Egyptians were obsessed with the eternal preservation of the divine king's *ka*, which in turn required the preservation of its natural home, his body. Hence the development of the celebrated Egyptian mummification process and the quest for permanent security in the conception of the tomb as the house for the *ka*: the repository of the body and the things it had used in this life – or, at least, of their images.

Unlike the ziggurat, the form was achieved pragmatically rather than with symbolic intent. As is evident from the section,[37] it evolved from a type of tomb cover called 'mastaba' – after the Arab word for a form of domestic bench which it resembled, though the mastaba itself doubtless derived from primitive houses of piled-up mud.[38] Beyond humanity, Djoser called for several mastabas to be superimposed then extended to produce a more memorable and impressive, more monumental form (the word 'monument'

36 Saqqara, mortuary complex of Djoser plan.

Its sides aligned with the cardinal directions, as with most of its descendants, the pyramid stood towards the centre of a rectangular compound – 547 by 278 metres (1795 by 912 feet) – enclosed by a stone wall. Buttressed in the regular way that early bricklayers probably derived from reed-bundle construction, this was punctuated by bastions, all but one of which had false doors. The sole entrance, in the south-east corner, led to a hall (1) with columns attached to its walls by stone spurs and roofed in imitation of parallel logs. Beyond this is a large court (2) flanked by a mastaba to the south (3) and the pyramid to the north (5) and containing pedestals and an altar (4). To the east of the court and the pyramid is a succession of smaller courts. The second from the south (6) was addressed by replicas of the chapels dedicated to the king's heb-sed festival and it is here that buildings of northern and southern type are to be distinguished (left and right respectively). The courts further north (7, 8) were addressed by palace halls representing Upper and Lower Egypt – the attached columns of the northern precinct still retain capitals reproducing the papyrus of the delta. Attached to the north side of the pyramid was the offering chapel (9), with false door, and the mortuary temple (10) before the opening of the passage down to the tomb chamber. This arrangement follows that of the more elaborate mastabas, though their entrance courts and mortuary chapels were usually on the east side.

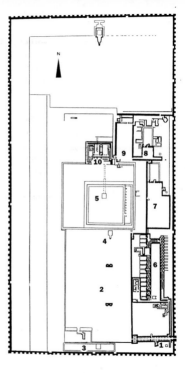

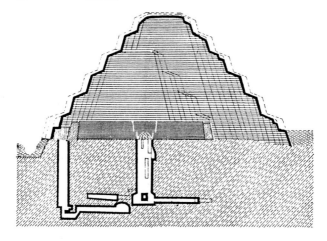

37 **Saqqara, mortuary complex of Djoser** section.

The earliest surviving monumental stone structure, this is also the earliest building attributable to a specific architect: Imhotep, the king's vizier, who may have conceived it and was certainly primarily responsible for the unprecedented organisation of labour and resources necessary to realise it. The section shows five stages in the development of its principal feature, the first pyramid: a conventional mastaba and its two enlargements; and the stepped superstructure and its enlargement, both of which consist of a core clad with several layers of inclined masonry to an ultimate length of 125 metres (410 feet), breadth of 109 metres (358 feet) and height of 60 metres (197 feet). The underground tomb chamber was enlarged and its entrance ramps changed several times as the project developed. Subsidiary chambers were provided for other members of the royal family.

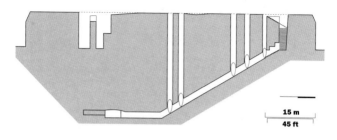

15 m
45 ft

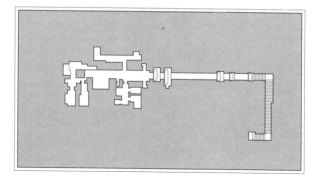

comes from the Latin for memorable, and the monumental relies on powerful simplicity for telling impact). This was an experimental procedure: multiplication to increase effect.

Like the ziggurat, Djoser's pyramid has no space inside it: the tomb chamber is excavated from the ground below, not encapsulated within the structure. However, an essential element in the conception was a false door in the blind wall of a chapel through which the *ka* could pass between the real and ideal spaces of this world and the stars. Above ground, the pyramid was the nucleus of a complex which reproduced the king's palace: the tomb, after all, is a house for eternity and here the ephemeral structures of this world were made eternal.

38 **Beit Khallaf, mastaba** III dynasty, section and plan.

Within a solid and unadorned brick slab, some 10 metres (33 feet) high, a staircase descends from the top to ground level near the northern end, continuing south below ground by an inclined ramp to a depth of some 20 metres (66 feet). At the base level, several tomb chambers are fed from a central corridor. Five vertical shafts punctuating the ramp allowed access to be blocked by inserted slabs of stone.

As the king was twice buried, this combination may reflect pre-dynastic burial practice in each kingdom: under the houses of the living in the agrarian north; in the sand of the desert beneath a tumulus in the recently nomadic south. In the simulated palace, moreover, the buildings associated with the government of Upper and Lower Egypt may be related to primitive prototypes: the tent of the south or the light reed structure derived from it; the reed-bundle hut of the delta or the brick structure which replaced it. The poles and canopy of the former are reproduced literally; the frame and stretched matting of the latter, fringed with fronds at the top, have been stylised as the torus-framed plane and cove cornice which were to be as typical of Egyptian architecture as reed-bundle columns. The rhythm of the buttresses which reinforce the brickwork in extended works like palace or city walls echoes the incidence of reed-bundle piers separated by matting, as in Sumer. As we have seen,

39 **Saqqara, mastaba of Mereruka and his family**
false door with statue of Mereruka.

Mereruka was vizier to Teti, the first king of the VI dynasty.

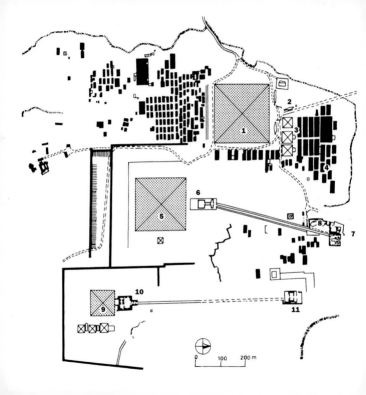

the hieroglyphs for the pharaoh's name include a palace façade – the place of appearance of the god-king among men (see 10, page 24). This is usually matched by the false door.[39]

In the dynasties when the sun god Re was in the ascendant, the combination of northern and southern types in the royal tomb complex was transformed. The southern tumulus was assimilated to the sacred mound of the northern centre of Heliopolis – the island on which Re alighted at the moment of creation – as a true prism. Symbolism rather than mere pragmatism is

40 **Gizeh, pyramid complexes of Khufu, Khafre and Menkaure** IV dynasty, site plan.

The Great Pyramid of Khufu (1) with the pits to the south and east in which the royal funerary barks were buried; the site of the mortuary temple (2) and end of the causeway from the valley temple; the pyramids of the queens and mastabas of members of the royal family (3); mastabas of dignitaries (4); the pyramid of Khafre (5) and its mortuary temple (6), causeway and valley temple (7); the sphinx (8); the pyramids of Menkaure and his queens (9), mortuary temple (10), causeway and valley temple (11). The equilateral sides of the pyramids face the cardinal directions.

41 **Gizeh, Great Pyramid of Khufu** section.

The largest of the pyramids was 230.5 metres (756 feet)
square and 146.5 metres (481 feet) high before it lost its
outer layer of dressed limestone. The mass is of limestone
blocks (weighing an average of 2.5 tonnes) in slender
vertical sections laid against a lightly battered core.
First excavated below the pyramid, the tomb chamber
was ultimately built into the main mass. The corridor to
the original chamber, entered from the north above ground
level, was deflected upwards and then ran parallel to
the ground to a second chamber – the so-called Queen's
Chamber, though it was also probably originally destined
for the king. From the point where the horizontal corridor
diverges from the inclined passage, the latter continues in
a great corbelled gallery 2 metres (6 feet 7 inches) wide and
28 metres (91 feet 10 inches) high to the chamber in which
Khufu was actually interred. Protected from the mass above
by superimposed tiers of stone beams, the top ones forming
a protean triangle, this is clad in granite and was sealed with
three granite portcullises in an antechamber.

Little is left of the offering chapel and mortuary temple,
axially aligned in the centre of the east side, or of the valley
temple, from which the bark carrying the royal coffin would
have processed along the causeway to the tomb. Enough of

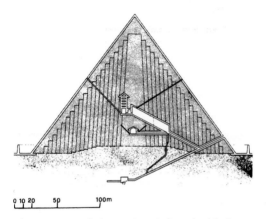

0 10 20   50   100m

the mortuary temple does survive to indicate that it had a
broad court surrounded by cloisters of square granite piers.
Opposite the entrance from the causeway, the piers were
tripled in a central recession to form a hypostyle hall before
the inner sanctum. On either side of the temple are pits for
the interment of the day and night barks which were to
carry the king eternally across the heavens with his father
Re. A pair of such barks was recovered virtually intact from
the pits to the south of the pyramid.

42 **Sunburst over the north African steppe.**

apparent as the generator of this form for the pyramids of the IV-dynasty pharaohs Sneferu at Dahshur and Khufu (Cheops) and his successors at Gizeh.[40-41] Dramatic manifestations of the sun's rays as a prism are common in north Africa[42] and it is not hard to see a stone prism as the petrification of the rays of the sun as well as an idealised island.[43]

Stars were identified with those who had passed to eternal glory, and the distribution of the three pyramids at Gizeh reflects the configuration of the main stars in the constellation of Orion, which is identified with Osiris. It also seems that the tiny shaft connecting the king's burial chamber to the outside is aligned with Orion, so the pyramid, whose form reflected the pharaoh's god-head in the sun, may also have provided a base for his *ka* to ascend to commune with the progenitor in the realm of the immortals, manifest in the stars.

The simulated palace was dispensed with, but its essential elements – the aisled hall of approach, the court of audience and the king's chamber – were

43 OVERLEAF **Gizeh, pyramids of Menkaure, Khafre and Khufu.**

44 Gizeh, Great Sphinx of Khafre with Great Pyramid of Khufu.

The sphinx is a syncretic creature of royal protection, invariably with the body of a lion and often with the head of a king, though sometimes with the head of the animal sacred to the god whose temple it guards.

retained for a mortuary temple enshrining the *ka* door
and dedicated to the veneration of the god-king's iden-
tity in Re, and for another temple in the valley where
the bark bearing the royal coffin left the river to continue its journey along the causeway to the tomb.
Beyond mummification, the valley temple catered for
the rites of the king's transformation into Osiris, with
which his responsibility for governing this world
passed to his son, the new Horus. Beside the grandest
of the valley temples, that of Khafre, the approach to
the pharaoh's last abode was guarded by his own
image endowed with the prowess of a lion: we shall
find no more arresting image of the king as divine protector than this Great Sphinx.[44]

From pyramid to temple

The endowment of a protective device with divine
symbolism was doomed to fail: it was effective only so
long as the pharaoh's sword was effective, but when
authority broke down the tombs were broken into and
robbed. The v-dynasty kings persevered with lesser

45 **Karnak, Great Temple of Amun, obelisk of Queen
Hatshepsut** c. 1460 BC.

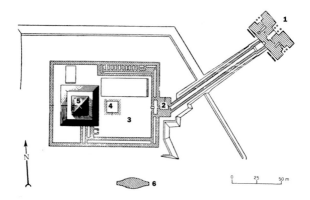

46 Abu Ghurab, sun temple of Neuserre V dynasty,
c. 2390 BC, plan and reconstructed view from the north.

As in the typical pyramid complex, the valley temple (1)
is linked by a causeway to the entrance to the main
temple, facing east (2). The large open court, surrounded
by corridors and magazines (3), contained an uncovered
altar (4) before the limestone obelisk on its battered base
(5), symbol of solar worship derived from the primeval

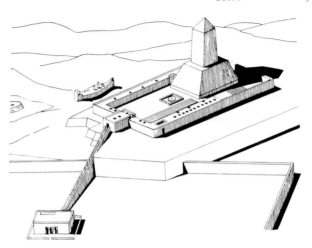

island upon which Re rested at the moment of creation.
To the south of the compound was a representation of
the solar bark in which Re daily crossed the heavens (6).
The form doubtless followed the sanctuary of Re at
Heliopolis, now lost.

pyramids, but also set the form on a massive tower and podium with battered sides as the central feature of a sun temple.[46] Elongated and refined, this was the prototype of the obelisk on which later ages were to raise the primeval mound towards the realm of the sun after Re had been absorbed by Amun. One of the largest marks the site of the sanctuary of Re at Heliopolis, but the form was also appropriated for the temples of Amun at Luxor and Karnak.[45]

The last pyramids of the Old Kingdom were insubstantial, and the rock-cut tombs of noblemen outdid the royal tomb, as their power eroded the pharaoh's state. On the revival of that state, the symbolic pyramid was eclipsed by the temple built for the ceremonies involved in the interment of the king. Their remains are scanty except for the mortuary complex of Nebhepetre-Mentuhotep, the Theban ruler who reunified Egypt c. 2060 BC. Here the elements of the old valley temple were elaborated, and despite a pyramid on one of its terraces, the tomb was buried in the rock under the hall.

Consciously emulating the work of Mentuhotep on an even grander scale at the same site, the first great mortuary complex of the New Kingdom was built by

Queen Hatshepsut (1473–1458 BC) for her father, her husband and herself.[47–49] This remarkable woman, who extended regency for her stepson (Tuthmosis III) into a personal reign of great cultural significance, dispensed with the pyramid altogether and concealed the tombs in the valley beyond the great spur to the north of her temple.

All later pharaohs hid their tombs beyond anonymous shafts, unmarked by any monumental form, in ravines such as the Valley of the Kings opposite Thebes. But the ruse is known to have worked in only one case: the tomb of the boy-king Tutankhamun (c. 1333–1323 BC), whose very insignificance was an important factor in ensuring his survival. At the end of the tunnel, room on room stored the king's effects, box in box contained three sarcophagi which reproduced his features. The outer two were of timber and gold, the solid-gold innermost one (see 11, page 30) contained his mummified body, and that, finally, was protected by the celebrated gold death mask.

Hatshepsut's greatest successors developed the mortuary temple for the worship of their deified *ka*, assimilating it to the temples of other manifestations of divinity. Beyond the forbidding entrance pylon

47 Deir el-Bahri, mortuary temples of Nebhepetre-Mentuhotep (2061–2010 BC) and Hatshepsut (1473–1458 BC) plan.

Preceded by a sacred grove, Mentuhotep's complex was laid out on two terraces. The first (1), projecting forward over a portico of square piers, carried the platform of the second on a solid central core surrounded by colonnades and a thick battered wall which, in turn, was flanked by galleries of more square piers on its three outer sides (2). On the inner side, the first terrace was extended back into the cliff on axis to the north-west, where it supported a court and hall of ten (or perhaps eleven) rows of eight octagonal columns before the inner sanctum (5). From the centre of the court (4), a ramp led down to the tomb chamber excavated from the solid rock under the cliff. It is thought that the second terrace was crowned by a small symbolic pyramid (3).

Dedicated to Amun, Hatshepsut's mortuary temple was approached from a valley temple along an avenue of sphinxes and through a vast forecourt (6) planted with a sacred grove – like Mentuhotep's earlier complex. There were three terraces, the lower two with porticos of square columns, the upper one supported by colonnades around the forecourt of the main sanctuary of Amun (13).

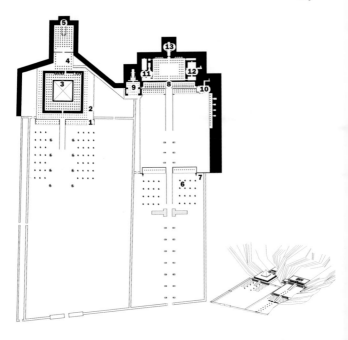

and colonnaded court, whose origins are represented in the works of the Old Kingdom at Saqqara and Gizeh (see 36, 40, pages 95, 102), the hall of many columns is the main new element in this definitive elaboration of the temple complex – as at Karnak[50-51] (built and rebuilt over more than 1500 years from c. 1800 BC) and Philae (built when Karnak was nearing completion) (see 22, pages 68–69).

The earliest-known hypostyle hall of stone completes Mentuhotep's mortuary temple. The origin of the form is explicit in the tent-pole columns of the heb-

The lower portico terminates in colossal statues of the queen as Osiris (7), and similar statues stand before the square piers of the higher portico (8). On that level, the mortuary chapels of the queen, her father and her husband (Tuthmosis I and II) were arranged to the left of the court (11) and to the right was a sanctuary dedicated to Re (12). On either side of the second terrace were sanctuaries of Hathor (the mother goddess, 9) and Anubis (guardian deity of burial places and patron of the mummification process, 10). The temple is attributed to the queen's steward, Senmut. It is embellished with some of the most superb reliefs to have survived from ancient Egypt.

48 **Deir el-Bahri, mortuary temples of Nebhepetre-Mentuhotep and Hatshepsut** view from the east.

49 OVERLEAF **Deir el-Bahri, mortuary temples of Nebhepetre-Mentuhotep and Hatshepsut** axonometric.

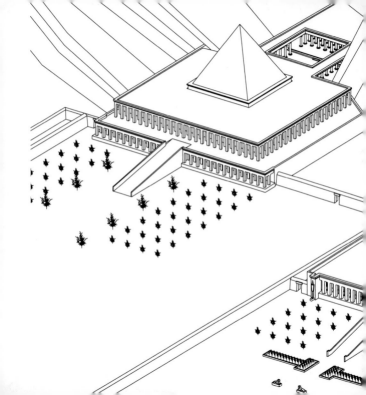

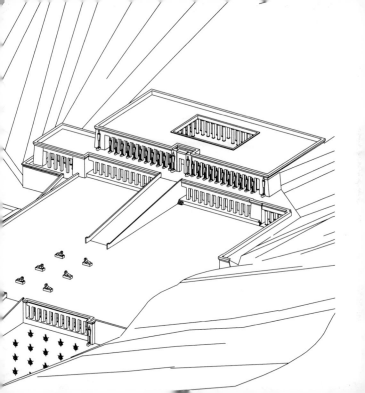

sed festival hall built by Tuthmosis III for the royal regeneration ceremony beyond the sanctuary of Amun at Karnak.[52] The greatest examples are those achieved by Ramesses II before that sanctuary and the sanctuary of Amun at Luxor:[53–54] the distinction of the high central nave from the side aisles apparent in the former was perpetuated in the form later adopted for the Roman basilica. If the temple stands for the sacred island, the hypostyle hall transcends its origins as a tent and stands for the sacred grove of primeval vegetation, its reed- or palm-shaped columns supporting a deep-blue ceiling spangled with stars.

Exceptional is the Great Temple of Ramesses II carved from the rock at Abu Simbel. There is no inner court, the hall is reduced to a minimum and the most powerful impression is made by the restricted passage to the sanctum, where colossal statues of the king as

50 **Karnak, Great Temple of Amun** view along the main axis.

An avenue of ram-headed sphinxes (mostly XXI dynasty) guards the king's way from the river to the first pylon. The image of the king usually borne by the sphinx is here replaced by the head of Amun's sacred ram.

51 Karnak, Great Temple of Amun plan of the precinct, with detail of the hypostyle hall clerestory (LEFT) and section through the Temple of Khons (OVERLEAF).

The grandest of all Egyptian temples, little survives of the original foundations of the XII-dynasty pharaoh Senwosret I except parts of the inner sanctuary (1) and a chapel reconstructed to the north of the great hypostyle hall from original elements used as infill in pylons dating from the end of the XVIII dynasty. The present complex was begun in the reign of Tuthmosis I. Enriched by successive XVIII-dynasty pharaohs with votive offerings in thanks for victories won under the auspices of the great Theban god, it was still being embellished after Egypt had been incorporated into the Roman empire.

The main axis runs east–west at right angles to the river in accordance with traditional practice. Nowhere better illustrates the typical Egyptian cult progression straight through varied spaces, diminishing in scale and light, to the intimacy of the inner sanctum. A secondary axis, parallel to the Temple of Khons in the south-west corner of the compound (14), leads south to the Temple of Mut. A gate opposite the entrance to the Khons shrine opens on to an avenue of rams and sphinxes which bypasses the sanctuary of Mut and runs on to Luxor in southern Thebes.

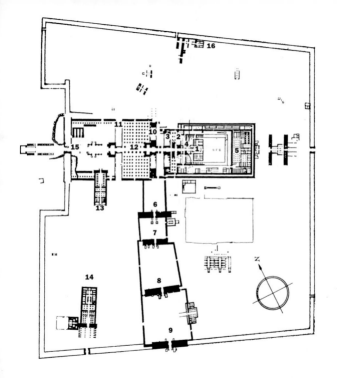

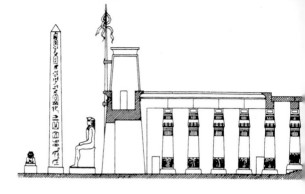

Tuthmosis I (1504–1492 BC) was responsible for the earliest surviving pylons (2, 3), four obelisks before the outer one (of which only one remains standing) and the hall between them. In front of the inner pylon (2) Queen Hatshepsut (1473–1458 BC) inserted two more obelisks, of which one remains standing (see 45, page 113).

Tuthmosis III (1479–1425 BC) built the innermost pylon (4), the court before it and the vestibule and chapel before the inner sanctum for the solar bark (acquired from Re) on which the statue of Amun was carried in processions. Beyond a court behind the sanctum, he erected a separate

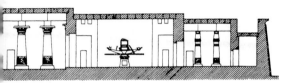

temple for his heb-sed festival: the principal element is a hypostyle hall modelled on a great marquee, with a nave of 24 columns perpendicular to the main axis of the complex and rising above square piers on all four sides (5).

Tuthmosis III (or Hatshepsut) opened the southern axis with two courts and pylons (6, 7), aligned with the outer entrance obelisks of Tuthmosis I. The southern axis was continued with two further courts and pylons (8, 9) by Horemheb (1319–1307 BC).

Meanwhile, Amenhotep III (1391–1353 BC) added another massive pylon to the west of the obelisks of

Tuthmosis I (10), and Horemheb added yet another (11) further west. Between these pylons, Seti I (1306–1290 BC) and Ramesses II (1290–1224 BC) installed the most impressive element of the whole complex: the great hypostyle hall of 134 papyrus columns (12). The central 12, rising to 21 metres (69 feet) to lift the nave roof above the level of the side aisles and admit light through a clerestory, have open-flower capitals; the columns of the 16 aisles rise to 13 metres (43 feet) and have closed-bud capitals.

The avenue of sphinxes leading from the river is mainly attributable to the XXI dynasty. Never completed, the outermost pylon (15) was probably also conceived under the XXI dynasty, though much of the structure seems to date from the XXX dynasty. In the north-west corner of the first court – substantial elements of which date from the XXV dynasty – is the bark shrine of Seti I. Breaching the southern wall is a complete miniature temple for the bark (13) built by Ramesses III (1194–1163 BC). Elsewhere in the precinct of Amun are numerous other chapels and shrines, of which the most important are the Temple of Ptah to the north (16) and Temple of Khons to the south (14 and section, PREVIOUS PAGES). Beyond the south pylon was an avenue of sphinxes along which the god progressed on the solar bark on his annual visit in the season of the flood to Luxor.

**52 Karnak, Great
Temple of Amun,
heb-sed festival hall
of Tuthmosis III** view
from nave to aisles.

The columns of
this putative basilica
reproduce the slender
wooden poles of the
traditional Egyptian
canopy in monumental
masonry. The origin
of the multi-columned
hall in the many-poled
marquee (and beyond
that, of the palace in
the camp of many
tents) is nowhere more
explicit.

53 **Karnak, Great Temple of Amun, great hypostyle hall of Seti I and Ramesses II** view from nave to aisles showing papyrus columns with open-flower and closed-bud capitals.

54 **Luxor (southern Thebes), Great Temple dedicated to Amun in the aspect of the fertility god Min**.

Built largely under Amenhotep III on the site of an earlier shrine, an outer court and pylons were added on a divergent axis by Ramesses II. To the south of the hypostyle hall and its court, with their exemplary papyrus-bundle and closed-bud columns, the sanctuary is preceded by new elements in the temple scheme: a shrine for the bark on which the god made his journey and a 'birth house' celebrating Amun's paternity of the founder.

55 Abu Simbel, Great Temple of Ramesses II

c. 1290 BC, interior of main passage.

Note the Osiris statues of the pharaoh attached to the piers. The temple was moved at vast expense to a new site further up the cliff during the construction of the Aswan High Dam.

56 OVERLEAF Abu Simbel, Great Temple of Ramesses II
façade.

Colossal statues of the founder are accompanied by
smaller ones of members of the royal family. The relatively
low door beneath the relief of Re in the centre of the pylon-
like façade – 35 metres (115 feet) wide by 32 metres (105
feet) high – leads to the hall of piers with attached colossal
statues of the king as Osiris and reliefs commemorating the
king's victories as a warrior. The main sanctuary, beyond
an inner hall and vestibule, contains statues of Ptah, Amun,
the king himself and Re which are lit by the rising sun twice
a year.

The prominence given to the Memphite and Heliopolitan
gods Ptah and Re beside Amun, the inclusion of the king
among them, his repeated representation in the passage
as Osiris, divine conqueror of death, and on the façade
as super-human among men after the example set by
Amenhotep III at Memnon in particular, are characteristic
of the XXI dynasty's reassertion of the king's divinity in
challenge to the power of the priests of Karnak. A smaller
temple nearby, dedicated to Hathor, likewise exalted
Ramesses II's queen, Nefertari.

Osiris stand in sinister sentinel.[55] Daunting as these are, nothing in the history of architecture asserts exclusivity more persuasively, or the pretensions of the patron more potently, than the giant images which flank the tiny entrance at the front[56] – except perhaps the Great Sphinx (see 44, pages 110–11).

The palace

The 'basilican' columned hall, like the great hypostyle hall of Seti I and Ramesses II at Karnak, was the major element of the palace, too. The remains of the principal residence of Amenhotep III at el-Malqata (west Thebes),[57] supplemented by those of the main palace of his successor Akhenaton at Akhetaton, provide a rare image of how the pharaoh lived at the height of ancient Egyptian civilisation.

At el-Malqata the main halls were all aisled basilicas. In the outer two, for public and restricted audience, the nave was dominated by a throne opposite the entrance; the innermost hall, flanked by the apartments of queens and princesses, led to a throne room before the king's own antechamber, bedroom and bathroom. Akhenaton's ceremonial palace had a double-aisled basilica to the south of the main court

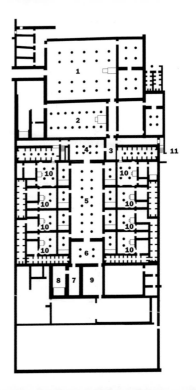

57 **el-Malqata (west Thebes), Palace of Amenhotep III** plan of the king's quarters.

Thought to have been the principal residence of the most opulent of the Egyptian kings, the complex as a whole consisted of several autonomous units with courts, halls and pavilions disposed to the north, east and south of a great court entered from the west. The general arrangement was somewhat organic, with great ceremonial halls and the palatine temple to the north, private apartments to the south and the servants in between, but the main units were formal in themselves.

Entrance to the first hall of the king's personal quarters
(1) was from the west through a corridor linked to a
neighbouring range of buildings south of the main court.
This hall was probably divided into a nave and aisles by
four rows of columns. A throne dominated the nave from
its eastern end, opposite the entrance. Another corridor
led from the southern corner of the hall, along the end of
another columned basilican throne room (2), to a vestibule
(3) at the eastern end of a third columned hall (4), parallel
to the others. After a third right-angle turn in the centre
of this third hall, the main axis to the inner sanctum
of the palace was defined by a grand central hall (5),
presumably once rising to a greater height than the outer
ones. At its far end, a throne room (6) led to the king's
own apartment, which consisted of antechamber, bathroom
and bedroom (7–9). To either side of the central hall were
the apartments (10) of the principal women of the court,
the king's sisters and daughters, but apparently not the
quarters of his principal wife, Queen Tiy. Her palace (11)
was to the east of the king's quarters. The two were joined
at the vestibule, which opened on to the central axis via
a passage at right angles to it, and to the corridor from
the entrance hall. Column bases and door cills were of
stone, but otherwise the structure was of timber and mud

brick. All surfaces in the main spaces were plastered and frescoed.

After the reassertion of his divinity in the XVIII and XXI dynasties, the living pharaoh needed temporary accommodation when taking part in ceremonies associated with his own cult. The temporary palace in the mortuary complex of Ramesses III nearby at Medinet Habu, like that of Ramesses II further north, follows the same formula as the palace at el-Malqata, but on a smaller scale. In a fortified compound entered through twin-towered gates to the east and west, the temple conformed to the standard set for buildings of this type by Ramesses II, presumably after the example of Amenhotep III's mortuary temple, now lost. Two courts, each with pylons, precede a hypostyle hall and two smaller inner halls before the sanctuary. The outer court is also the forecourt to the small palace on its western side. On axis with the entrance and the 'window of appearances' overlooking the court, a small hypostyle hall leads to the throne, behind which is a private audience chamber and living rooms.

and a vast hypostyle hall in a separate compound.[58]
The royal family's quarters, linked to the court by a
bridge over the main road, were set in a garden.

The house of Akhenaton's vizier Nakht was also a
villa in its own garden.[59] A square, court-like room
was preceded by a great hall and surrounded by private suites on its other sides. Columns raised the
central room's roof above the level of the others to
admit light through windows in the superstructure
(clerestory). With less ground, especially on older-
established sites, the better houses would usually have
a vestibule, columned hall and reception room with
clerestory, backed or flanked by bedrooms and bathrooms and aligned to the south of a portico and
entrance court.

58 **Akhetaton (Tell el Amarna), Palace of Akhenaton,
central ceremonial and administrative area** plan.

(1) Ceremonial palace with great court to the north,
flanked by the so-called harem buildings on the east and the
audience hall and ancillary spaces (centre), with the great
festival hall to the south; (2) the king's private quarters;
(3) palatine Temple of Aton; (4) Great Temple of Aton;
(5) storehouses; (6) offices; (7) barracks.

1

2

3

4

5

6

7

N

300 m.

In palaces, as in temples, the main spaces were embellished with images representing their use. Less formal rooms were elegantly decorated with motifs
drawn from nature, especially the flora and fauna of
the river. Even floors were plastered and painted, often
with a pool surrounded by reeds with birds and animals, as in a garden.[60] The garden itself introduces all
the features of formal landscaping to be developed

**59   Akhetaton, Palace of Akhenaton, house of the vizier
Nakht** reconstructed plan.

Entrance is through two vestibules and three right-angle
turns to the main reception hall (1); at right angles to this
hall and aligned with the central bay of its colonnade – as
in the core of the Palace of Amenhotep III (see 57, page 139) –
is the central living/dining room (2) with its large divan
platform and smaller washstand; flanking and insulating
this central space, in addition to service rooms and
storehouses, was a second hall to the west (3) and a
withdrawing room to the south (4) between two apartments
– as in the palace, these consisted of antechambers,
bathrooms and bedrooms (5–7). The staircase obviously
implies a second storey, presumably of rooms for other
members of the family.

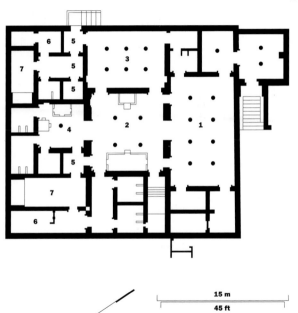

15 m

45 ft

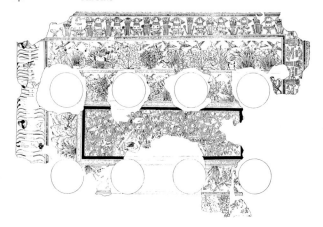

60 **Akhetaton, Palace of Akhenaton, central ceremonial area** drawing of painted floor from the 'harem' range.

61 **Thebes, tomb of an official in the reign of Amenhotep III** drawing of a fresco representing an enclosed garden.

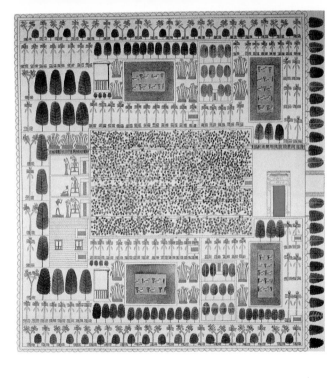

over the following three millennia: regular enclosure;[61] plants, useful as well as beautiful, set in ordered rows and clipped to regular forms (topiary); a central axis with symmetrical paths; pools for irrigation and fish; a framework for climbing plants to provide shade (pergola); and statues representing the gods presiding over a special place descended from the sacred grove, the scene of the mystery of growth, of the provision of food and medicine, where people confronted the forces of nature over which they had little control but upon which they depended for their existence.

Early towns are always composed of many walled complexes; it is the arteries of communication between them – the streets and squares – that may reveal urban order. But order is certainly not characteristic of primitive settlements. Before planning guidelines can be imposed, the development of towns is organic: it follows the tracks made by feet taking the lines of least resistance provided by the contours of the site – as at Catal Huyuk (see 4, page 13), Ur (see 25, page 75) and, no doubt, earliest Memphis and Thebes. And as we have seen, when building with walls there is no incentive to impose an overall formality on the distribution of spaces because it can never be seen.

Egypt: grids and zoning

A new town on a fresh site, Akhetaton (mid 14th century BC) seems to have been planned with a dominant artery and something of a grid in its centre, though its development along the river seems to have obviated further order. No doubt the grid took the temples and palaces as its point of departure (see 58, page 143) – though it is obviously efficient to provide regular blocks for houses without awkward junctions or irregularly shaped spaces. One hundred and

62 Medinet Habu (northern Thebes), town remains north of the tomb of Ramesses III.

After Amenhotep III established himself opposite Luxor at el-Malqata, western Thebes began to eclipse the old town on the east bank of the river. Under the XIX dynasty its centre was about a kilometre north-east of el-Malqata at Medinet Habu.

50 m

150 ft

fifty years later a grid asserts itself even over the dilapidated remains of the houses built for the workers of Ramesses III at Medinet Habu (northern Thebes).[62]

Five hundred years earlier, the new town of Senwosret II at el-Lahun[63] was not only built on a grid but was divided into walled zones with standardised housing for the different classes of society. The officials' houses anticipated those of Akhetaton but the cells of the workers fell well short of the standard achieved early in the 15th century BC at Deir-el-Medineh.[64] Doubtless knowing of el-Lahun, the Greek historian Herodotus noted that a pharaoh called Sesostris (Senwosret) divided the whole country into square plots for purposes of taxation. Regular division certainly dates from the Egyptian Old Kingdom, though not necessarily using square plots.

63 **el-Lahun** XII dynasty, plan.

(1) Acropolis with ruins of the governor's establishment, perhaps occupied by the king on visits to supervise the construction of his pyramid nearby; (2) western quarter with the grand houses of the administrators; (3) cellular eastern quarter with back-to-back houses for the workers.

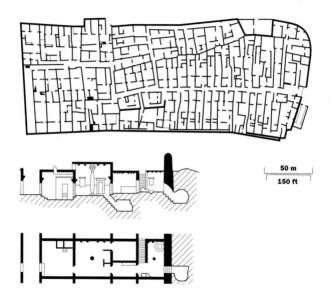

50 m
150 ft

Babylon

Most Mesopotamian towns followed the pattern of Ur
(see 25, page 75), though in late Babylon the definition of
the blocks is more disciplined, if not quite as ordered
as in the new towns of Egypt. Long settled and peri-
odically redeveloped on either side of the Euphrates,
the site reveals both organic growth and regular planning. Herodotus describes the streets as straight, some
parallel and some perpendicular to the river, and
excavation confirms that the main streets of the town
of Nebuchadnezzar II (605–562 BC) were more or less
parallel or perpendicular to the ceremonial axis from
the palace to the Temple of Marduk – probably the
grandest thoroughfare of pre-Roman antiquity.[65]

64 **Deir-el-Medineh** plan of workers' village with section
and plan of a typical house.

The settlement seems to have been founded at the outset
of the XVIII dynasty to house the workers on the tombs of
Amenhotep I and Tuthmosis I in the Valley of the Kings.
The standard of workers' housing set at Deir-el-Medineh,
with rooms aligned end to end and lit from narrow alleys at
the side, represents a marked improvement over the back-
to-back cells of el-Lahun.

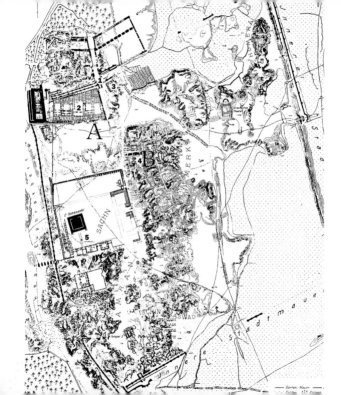

Little survives of the principal temples – the Temple of Ishtar in the north near the gate which bears her name (see 18, pages 60–61), the Temple of Shamash in the south, the Temple of Adad in the west and the Temple of Marduk in the centre – but there is enough to indicate that their plans conformed to ancient tradition. And as of old, the Palace of Nebuchadnezzar II was a warren of rooms around regular courts.

Dur-sarrukin

Grand as this must have been, it hardly surpassed the latest works of the Assyrians – and it was the complex of palace, temple and ziggurat on the vast terrace that

65 **Babylon** plan of royal and ceremonial centre and district east of the Euphrates as rebuilt after the restoration of the kingdom towards the end of the 7th century BC.

(1) Ishtar Gate; (2) Palace and hanging gardens of Nebuchadnezzar II; (3) Temple of Nin-Makh; (4) Temple of Ishtar and residential quarter; (5) central cult enclosure of Esagila with the ziggurat (to the north) and Temple of Marduk (to the south, beyond the line of the surviving walls of the vast compound which once embraced it too).

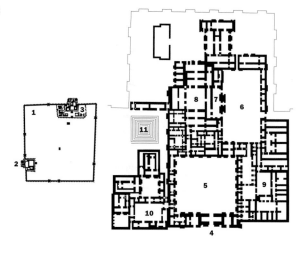

66 Dur-sarrukin (Khorsabad), Palace of Sargon II
(722–705 BC), plan with block plan of town inset and reconstructed view

Roughly square, the area enclosed by the town walls (1) covered nearly 2.6 square kilometres (a square mile). Development within it was far from complete when the new

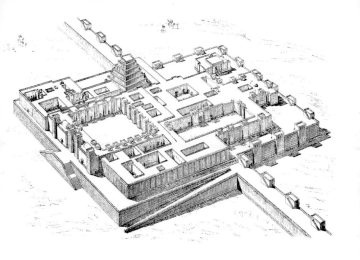

capital was abandoned after its founder's early death in 705. The walls were buttressed with regular projections and pierced with seven gates, two in each range except the north-west. The main gate (2), towards the southern corner facing in the direction of Kuyunjik (Nineveh), was guarded by a fort on a platform, as was the main palace. The main citadel, containing the official and cult buildings – within the urban area but on a higher level – was incorporated within the town defences towards the northern corner (3). Rising out of it on a great platform, equal to the height of the walls and projecting beyond them, was the king's palace. The buildings within the citadel were distributed informally and, contrary to the ideal reconstruction shown here but as in the block plan, the palace was not plotted on a rectangular grid – for reasons which remain obscure.

A ramp led from the central square of the citadel, where the king would appear before the masses, to the main twin-towered portal of the palace (4). Flanked by subsidiary entrances, this was guarded by winged bulls with human heads (see 67, page 162) – like several others in the complex and in other palaces of Assyria. All three gatehouses led straight through to the outer court of the palace (5), where those seeking or summoned to audience presumably assembled. From the northern corner of the outer court restricted access was gained to the southern corner of the great audience court (6). More nearly rectangular than the outer court, this was dominated from the centre of its south-western side by another twin-towered portal flanked by subsidiary doors. These led on axis to the throne room (7):

the throne, if not set in the central arch to command large
gatherings outside, stood before the end wall to the left.
Two further right-angle turns, into and out of a corridor,
led slightly off axis to the king's apartment, centred on the
court of private audience (8), and to the rooms of his
women. To the right of the outer court was the service zone
(9). To the left was a complex of temples (10). Behind this,
adjacent to the royal apartments, was a ziggurat formed by
a continuous ramp: if its height matched its breadth at base
– 45 metres (148 feet) – it had seven stages (11).

   The walls throughout the complex were built of brick
with voussoir arches. Many spaces were vaulted, but the
throne room probably had a ceiling of expensive imported
timber. Around the walls of the main ceremonial spaces,
beyond the great guardian monsters, ran a dado of stone
slabs (orthostats) with reliefs celebrating the majesty and
prowess of the king. In the temple complex the dado was
revetted with glazed bricks with sacred animals, birds,
plants and symbols in low relief. Above the dados and
elsewhere walls were plastered. Important rooms were
painted with images of the king and his attendants in
framed arches over heraldic friezes. The palace was
comprehensively drained through terracotta conduits in
the platform.

67 Dur-sarrukin, Palace of Sargon II, pair of winged, human-headed bulls (Lamassu).

The creatures guard the palace from the intrusion of evil. As these figures are represented in deep relief, to be viewed orthogonally from the front and the sides of the portal arch, they appear to have five legs when seen obliquely from the corner. Syncretic images of the power of the king, high priest of Ashur, they are invariably dominated Sargon II's new capital, Dur-sarrukin (c. 705 BC),[66] that brought the tradition of early palace and temple architecture to its apogee. Never have there been more potent icons of royal prowess than the Lamassu[67] – the great syncretic monsters which guarded the portals with the fierceness of the lion, the far-sightedness of the eagle, the strength and endurance of the bull, and the wisdom and intelligence of man – except for the sphinxes of the pharaohs.

accompanied by sacred protective genii carrying a pot of holy water and a sprinkler (see 15, page 46) or sacrificial animals and implements (as here).

Lamassu were found at the doors of the major 1st-millennium Assyrian palaces at Kuyunjik (Nineveh) and Kalhu (Nimrud) as well as Dur-sarrukin. They guarded the royal gates with lions and the syncretic sphinx, presumably borrowed from Egypt.

It was the Hittites, borrowing from the Egyptians probably through Syria, who provided the Assyrians with the precedent for the Lamassu: the gates of their ruggedly defended towns were guarded by lions and sphinxes – visible sometimes from the side as well as the front.[69-70] Generally unrefined,[68] their buildings reveal an order foreign even to the Assyrians but comparable to that of the Trojans, who settled earlier in Anatolia, and may well have been distant Aryan relatives.

Like other early Anatolian settlements, Hissarlik (ancient Troy) was a citadel with palatial buildings but little that obviously represented a religious sanctuary. The formidable Hittite capital at Hattusas (Boghazkoy) was dominated by a citadel from the outset, though many temples were built below it in the 14th century BC and later. Of the citadel palace, nothing remains above foundation level. Of several temples, the bases of walls reveal at least the plan.

The main compound of so-called Temple 1 is assertively rectilinear, in contrast with the ranges of magazines surrounding it, and is entered from a cen-

68 **Hattusas, access gallery of cyclopean masonry**
through the Yerkapu hill below the southern sphinx gate.

69 Hattusas (Boghazkoy), lion gate.
The Hittite capital was defended from the 14th century
BC by some 6 kilometres (4 miles) of doubled walls. Built
of stone and punctuated regularly by towers, these were
based on earth mounds (glacis) faced with stone. Concealed
tunnels with corbelled vaults of cyclopean masonry
provided access through the glacis. The twin-towered
south-western gate protected the outer town. In the absence
of evidence for earlier practice at the old Assyrian capital
of Ashur, it is assumed that the conception of the Lamassu
derived from the Hittites. Note here that only the foreparts
of the lions are revealed before the jambs.

70 **Alaca Huyuk, sphinx gate to the citadel** 14th century BC. Note the double-headed eagle carved towards the base of the jambs.

At Hattusas, the Yerkapu hill to the south of the city had a gate with winged sphinxes, more delicately carved than the lions of the south-western gate and represented from the side as well as the front. The sphinx was probably imported into Anatolia from Syria, where it had been taken by the Egyptians of the Middle Kingdom. It is known from surviving records of correspondence that 13th-century BC Hittite rulers borrowed sculptors from Babylon.

71 **Hattusas, 'Temple I'** c. 1350 BC, plan.

Set in the northern sector of the walled area of the town, this was a dual sanctuary of the great god of Hatti and his consort Arinna. (1) Circuit of magazines; (2) double portico with square piers facing out and into the main court; (3) so-called king's chamber, probably for ritual washing and/or dining; (4) twin shrines. It is known from surviving records that the king officiated at certain religious ceremonies, processing into the precinct through the royal gate, washing his hands, seating himself on a throne and sharing a ritual meal with the gods. With windows even in the walls of the main shrines, the sanctuary was defended by the closed circuit of magazines.

Above a rough stone base and dressed vertical slabs (orthostats), the structure of most Hittite buildings was of sun-dried brick reinforced with timber. The technique seems to have originated in northern Syria, where it was used in the 18th century BC for the Palace of Yarimlim at Alalakh (Tell Archana). These orthostats are the ancestors of the panels illustrating royal ceremonial or heroic prowess in the Assyrian palaces (see 15–16, pages 46, 48–49).

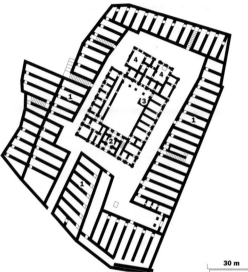

30 m
90 ft

72 **Hissarlik (ancient Troy)** plan of excavations of the
citadel by Schliemann (1870–90), Dörpfeld (1893–94)
and Blegen (1932–38) superimposing the phases of
development as levels I, II, VI (early 3rd millennium to late
2nd millennium BC) and later (the site was occupied for
nearly 2500 years).

Troy was a citadel rather than a city for most of its
history (following an Anatolian tradition that goes back
at least to Hacilar, c. 5400 BC, and is paralleled in Greece
after the foundation of Dimini in Thessaly c. 3000 BC).
Its battered walls were based on dressed stone from the mid
3rd millennium. Though contained by the earliest walls, the
four parallel buildings at the top, opposite the main gate
with back-to-back porches, probably formed the nucleus
of the second citadel palace, destroyed towards the end of
the 3rd millennium (see 73, page 172). The integrity of each
unit is noteworthy: megarons, all have a hall with a porch,
some have a false porch behind the hall, and one has a
vestibule between its porch and hall. With greater width
came the need for internal columns (two side by side in the
porches, several in a row in the largest of the early palace
buildings, as in the central structure to the south of level VI).
The earliest house excavated at the site has a hall and porch,
but little remains of any town around the citadel.

I

IIa

IIb

IIc-g

VI

IX

30 m

90 ft

73 **Hissarlik** overview of the megarons which probably formed the nucleus of the second citadel palace.

74 **Pylos (Englianos), Palace of Nestor** 13th century BC,
view into the king's chamber.

At the centre of an extensive complex, the megaron had
a porch and a circular central hearth flanked by the bases
of four columns. According to the *Iliad*, King Nestor of
Messenian Pylos provided the second-largest contingent of
Greek ships in the war against Troy.

tral portal.[71] With a tripartite vestibule between twin columned porticos facing out and in, the portal conforms to a recurrent type first found in the lower levels of Hissarlik.[72] Indeed, like the shrines at the head of the court, this is a variant of the porticoed hall (megaron) which constituted the Trojan palace.[73]

Porch and hall were also the basic constituents of early Bronze-Age houses in Anatolia: at Kanesh (Kultepe) in Cappadocia the remains of a palace conforming to the type with internal columns have been dated to the mid 3rd millennium BC. Across the Aegean in Thessaly, houses from the 4th millennium have been found with colonnaded porch, hall and storeroom between parallel walls, though the internal partition was not necessarily rectilinear and the back wall was sometimes curved. Most early Greek houses were probably horseshoe shaped at first – like caves, but perhaps derived from the circular hut with annex. The side walls were then straightened, the apsidal end screened off and then made rectangular (as at Hissarlik). The porch was optional and an anteroom appears only in the middle of the 2nd millennium. The grandest halls had hearths flanked by columns, but these did not appear until towards the end of the 3rd millennium.[74]

Arriving on the Aegean coast of Anatolia from east or west, the Aryans confronted one of the most seductive civilisations of the ancient world. It emanated from Crete, where important urban centres of power had developed long before Babylon first rose to prominence with Hammurabi. The earliest inhabitants possibly crossed from Asia Minor in the Ice Age, when the water in the Mediterranean was low, though similarities between early Cretan and Anatolian culture suggest that an important contingent at least may have come much later – at about the time of Catal Huyuk (8th to 7th millennia BC). The agglomeration of their irregular, flat-roofed houses had become towns by the middle of the 3rd millennium BC. Cultural assimilation through maritime contact was probably reinforced by immigration after the Hittite invasion.

Crete: a new civilisation

It was at the beginning of the 2nd millennium BC that the appearance of great palaces in the organic cities of Crete marked the advent of a new civilisation, specifically Cretan, though influenced by Mesopotamia. Its power was maritime and it felt so secure that its cities were undefended.[75] Its wealth was based on trade

between Egypt and the Phoenicians, Anatolians and Europeans. Its fertile valleys fostered a more diverse agriculture than topography permitted elsewhere in the Aegean area.

Minoan cosmology

Seeking harmony with cyclical nature, the religion of ancient Crete was centred on devotion to the mother goddess, patron of fertility, perhaps especially in her manifestation as the moon, mistress of animals. She married a sacrificial consort at each New Year regeneration festival. Excited to resurrection in phallic cults, the consort survived sacrifice as priest-king and found a surrogate in the bull, icon of male potency.[76-77] His symbol was the sacrificial axe with its double moon-shaped heads – the labrys. His ascendency is told in the legend of Minos – after whom the civilisation is called Minoan.

Minos was the son of the great sky god whom the later Greeks called Zeus. Zeus was the Cretan-born son of Kronos and Rhea – themselves the offspring of Uranus, king of the heavens, and the earth mother Gaia. Having gained supremacy, Zeus disguised himself as a bull to abduct the Phoenician princess Europa:

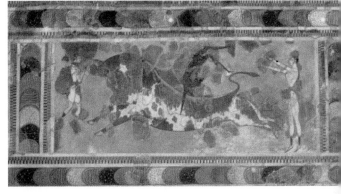

76 **Knossos, Palace of Minos, fresco from the north portico** c. 1600 BC, bull with leaping youths.

75 PREVIOUS PAGES **Thera (Santorini), fresco with Cretan palace-city** before 1500 BC (Athens, National Museum).

Note that the building, with its large windows and open terraces, is undefended from the sea. The volcanic island of Thera exploded c. 1500 BC.

77 Hagia Triada, fresco from a sarcophagus 14th century BC, bull sacrifice (Herakleion, Archaeological Museum).

Minoans slaughtered bulls in sacrifice, and bull leaping (see 76, page 179) was probably part of the preparatory rites that took place in the great court of Minos' palace at Knossos.

The most sacred ceremony of the Cretan calendar, central to the New Year festival as in Mesopotamia, was the remarriage of the priest-king to the mother goddess (the queen as priestess) which stood for the annual death and rebirth of the vegetation god. Minos was descended from the union of the mother goddess and her consort, whom he impersonated in the remarriage ceremony, but he was also the son of Zeus disguised as a bull, and the bull was his natural surrogate when his death and replacement ceded to remarriage each year.

The transition (and confusion) between the annual death of the priest-king and the sacrifice of his surrogate bull is well represented in the myth of the Minotaur: Poseidon (Zeus' brother, god of the sea) sent a bull for Minos to sacrifice; Minos found it too beautiful and sacrificed another; Poseidon, offended, caused Queen Pasaphae to fall in love with the bull and couple with it instead of the king; the Minotaur was the issue.

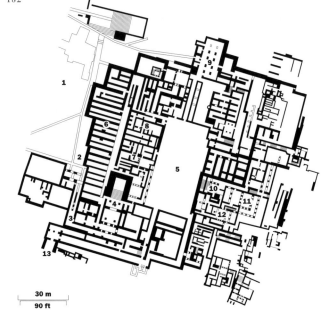

30 m

90 ft

Minos was the product of their union. Minos' wife, Queen Pasaphae, also coupled with a bull: the issue was the monstrous man-bull Minotaur. The later Greek legend of Theseus concerns Crete's subjection of Hellas (Greece) and exaction of a tribute of the flower of its youth to be devoured by the Minotaur in his incomprehensible labyrinth of Minos' palace at Knossos.

Knossos

There were several autonomous palatine cities on Crete, but Knossos, first built c. 2000 BC and rebuilt after a catastrophe c. 1700 BC, seems to have been the

78 **Knossos, Palace of Minos** largely rebuilt c. 1700 BC after incorporating parts of the palace begun three centuries earlier, plan.

(1) 'West court'; (2) western entrance; (3) 'corridor of the processions'; (4) portico and grand staircase to ceremonial rooms on the first floor; (5) great central court; (6) magazines; (7) pillared crypt below the ceremonial rooms; (8) 'throne room'; (9) northern entrance and portico; (10) royal apartments, main staircase; (11) 'hall of the double axes' in the king's quarters; (12) 'queen's suite'; (13) southern entrance.

Excavated and partially restored from 1900 by Sir Arthur Evans, who named its spaces, the palace is approached from the south over a viaduct and from the west up the 'Royal Road' or 'Sacred Way'. At the top of this route is a stepped platform for ceremonial performances (called the 'theatral area'), beyond which is the northern entrance (9). This leads through a grand pillared hall and corridor directly to the central court. The southern entrance (13) serves an extended corridor which turns through several right angles before reaching the central court.

The principal entrance to the state apartments in the west wing, known as the 'west court' (1), opens from the south-west corner of the piazza south of the 'theatral area' and west of the palace. This leads from a portico, with one column *in antis*, to a processional corridor which turns through a right angle towards a grand inner propylon. To the north of this was the ceremonial staircase to the great audience halls on the first floor (4). The stout walls supporting them, not necessarily related to the superstructure, enclosed the storage magazines and crypts. Two of the latter (7) contain stone pillars inscribed with the sacred labrys and flanked by shallow troughs to receive the libations of a fertility cult, doubtless involving the dedication of agricultural produce from the neighbouring stores at a harvest festival. To the north is the so-called 'throne room' (8). A splendid throne, flanked by benches, was found here, but addressing a sunken tank in an open court (one of several in the palace), it was probably for the king as priest officiating at a religious ceremony.

The royal apartments in the east wing are ranged on five levels connected by the magnificent staircase restored by Evans (10). At its foot, the 'hall of the colonnades' is joined by a corridor to the king's main living room (11) – called the 'hall of the double axes' by Evans because of the many labrys carved into its walls. Subdivided by piers, lit from a court to the west and connected with another suite to the south (called the 'queen's suite' without evidence), it opened through a colonnade on the east and south to a garden terrace and magnificent view of the valley below. There were similar suites upstairs.

The 'royal villa' to the west of the palace was built to a small scale and in a relatively short time in the late Minoan period. Not the product of organic growth, it was asymmetrical by design – if more formal than any other Minoan building.

The earliest houses in the town consisted of clustered rooms grouped haphazardly and, as at Catal Huyuk, some could be reached only over the roofs of their neighbours.

79 **Knossos, Palace of Minos** view through colonnade and over terrace to the countryside.

80 **Knossos, Palace of Minos** 'queen's suite' and adjoining colonnaded court.

seat of a pre-eminent secular, economic and religious authority. More completely organic than any in Mesopotamia and always growing, the palace[78] had three once-independent, well-drained, multi-storey zones about a great court. The western wing accommodated royal ceremonial and cult ritual, notably pillar worship, beside and above stores for agricultural reserves; the eastern one housed the king and his family; the north was divided between guests and servants. Outward-looking to the landscape and terraced to the contours of the site – like all Cretan towns – the flat-roofed agglomeration of rooms was served by circuitous corridors leading from the main entrance in the west and subsidiary entrances to the north and south. The pattern of walls is indeed labyrinthine, but with timber as well as stone and clay then available on Crete, space often flows through colonnaded screens, loggias and porticos.[79]

The central court, separating the public and private ranges, was overlooked from loggias and served as an arena for ritual contests such as bull leaping (see 76, page 179). Though the concept of the court was probably borrowed from Mesopotamia, it was not a place of assembly oriented to the rooms of state with precon-

ceived formality, but residual space encroached upon
by service rooms. Walls were habitually diversified in
plane, to avoid monotony. Above orthostats, also
Mesopotamian, decoration ignored integrity of form,
with frescos ramping freely around corners.[80-81] A
vivacious procession of tribute-bearers followed the
main corridor, but fish, birds and animals (real or
heraldic) and stylised plant motifs were predominant
– as they always were in communities dedicated to the
worship of the female principle.

The Cretans built with brick or rubble and used a
considerable amount of stone, at least on the ground
floors of their palaces. The flat roofs of large buildings were supported on a timber frame with rubble or
brick infill where stone was impractical. Columns

81 OVERLEAF **Knossos, Palace of Minos** 'throne room',
detail showing restored frescos with heraldic beasts.

With adjoining facilities for ritual libation, this room was
possibly the scene of the king's annual remarriage to the
mother goddess. It was rebuilt, or at least redecorated, in
the late Minoan period and, though based on fragmentary
evidence, the restoration conveys something of the palace's
late style.

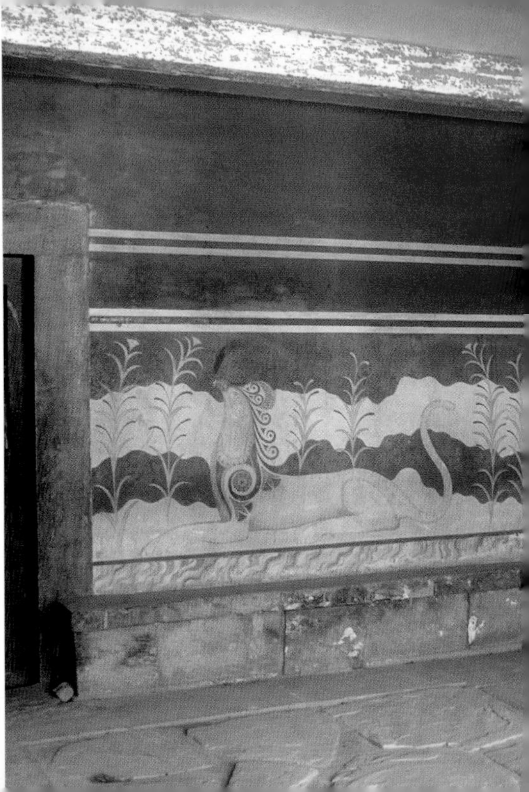

were usually of wood, the tree trunk dressed and inverted to taper down to the slot in a stone base. Thus the column presented its greater diameter to the load transmitted through the slab (abacus) and cushion (echinus) of its capital, also of wood. Abacus and echinus are separated by shallow grooves and the capital from the column by a ring moulding (astragal). Columns often alternate with rectangular piers. The most common decorative motifs were waves of interlaced spirals, rosettes, and rosettes split by spirals in vertical bands.

The Aryan invasions

Knossos and the other Minoan cities were destroyed around 1450 BC – perhaps by invaders, but most probably by natural cataclysm. Native Minoan civilisation failed to recover, though the palaces were rebuilt in part and occupied for another century by invaders from Greece. These invaders were called 'Mycenaean' after the stoutly fortified, lion-guarded seat of Agamemnon, the king who seems to have asserted suzerainty over them. Their ancestors were the Aryan speakers of an Indo-European language, later to develop as Greek, who infiltrated the Balkans in the previous millennium, or possibly crossed the Helle-spont from north-east Anatolia after establishing themselves at Troy. In either case, they may well have been the precursors of the Hittites.

The invaders had subjugated the indigenous Aegean inhabitants of Hellas (Greece) – who were related to the Cretans – from castles such as Myce-nae[82] by the 18th century BC, but were themselves overwhelmed in about 1500 BC by further waves of Aryans, generally called 'Achaeans'. However, they had mastered the sea, and it may have been the consequent turmoil which destroyed the Minoans. Patriarchal warriors and sky-god worshippers, the Aryans could hardly have been more different from the luxurious and genial earth mother-worshipping Aegean natives, whose superior culture must both have attracted and repelled them. The impact is a main concern of Greek mythology, especially the rape or marriage of the local queen, priestess and goddess by the tribal chief and his patron.

Internecine rivalry began to sap the Achaeans' strength in the 13th century BC, and though an Achaean contingent seems to have overcome Troy towards the middle of that century, they fell to invaders

from the north soon after. These were Aryans too, but armed with iron rather than bronze. Called 'Dorians', they swept their opponents down the Attic peninsula and out into the Aegean, where Achaean bands had long rampaged of their own accord and cohabited with the natives. A protracted process of Aryan infiltration reaching several climaxes seems more likely than shock invasions; whatever the case, the speakers of a primitive Greek dialect known as 'Doric' appear predominant in Hellas itself, especially in the Peloponnesus, after the mid 12th century BC, and a related

82 PREVIOUS PAGES **Mycenae** view from the south with the citadel (top) and outer defences of the surrounding settlement.

The citadel may have been founded as early as c. 1750 BC, but in the main dates from the mid 14th century. Sacked c. 1200 and partially rebuilt, it was destroyed again c. 1100.

83 **Mycenae, citadel entrance (lion gate)** after c. 1250 BC.

Note the massive stone lintel, corbelled tympanum and inset heraldic device with lions, and sacred pillar reproducing the Cretan type of column.

dialect, later called 'Ionic', spread from Attica to the islands and the coast of Asia Minor.

Mycenae and Tiryns

Ideologically relevant as Minoan ornament was, it masks, rather than elucidates, the realities of building. The Achaeans employed Cretan artists, but their obsession with logic, which they brought to the comprehension of the order of creation, determined their own approach to decoration and planning: to the organisation of space and the articulation of mass in terms of structure.

On the portal of the great fortress at Mycenae,[83] the dominant element is obviously heraldic: the lion is a ubiquitous symbol of royal power, as important to the Hittites as the eagle, and the pillar is the age-old male fertility-cult object which we found specially accommodated in the crypts of Knossos. It is hard to imagine florid ornament concealing the structure at Mycenae – on the contrary, the great stone walls are seen to support a massive lintel over the entrance and, limiting the pressure on the lintel, the courses of masonry above are corbelled. A symbolic device is slotted into the cavity left by the structure: ornament disciplined by building.

As to planning, it is equally logical to think in terms of planar geometry, of axial alignment, not to leave things to whim but to impose order. This is characteristic of the Achaeans – and of their cousins the Trojans and their remote relatives the Hittites. Their citadel palaces were dominated by one big hall, which was the standard unit of pre-Hellenic residential accommodation, possibly derived from the cave. Homer's megaron, this was preceded by a vestibule and/or portico, as at Troy (see 72, page 171), and had a central hearth flanked by four columns. The Achaeans do not seem to have had temples, only open-air altars. Their tombs, recalling the most primitive form of Aryan hut derived from the tent, consisted of a circular chamber with a corbelled dome in the shape of a beehive on axis with a long passage.[84]

The best-preserved Achaean citadel, begun c. 1400 BC and destroyed three centuries later, is at Tiryns.[85-86] Entrance is via a ruggedly corbelled passage skirting cyclopean walls,[87] via a right-angle turn into the rectangular outer court and then, after another sharp turn, through the off-centre gate into the square inner court. Dominating this court from the centre of the north side, opposite an open-air altar, is the main ele-

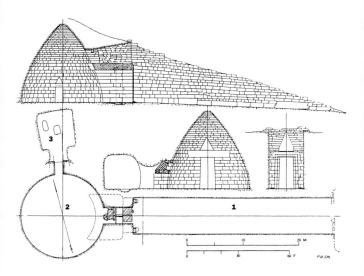

0   10   20 M
0   30   60 F

Palox.

84 **Mycenae, 'Tomb of Agamemnon' or 'Treasury of Atreus'** possibly c. 1250 BC, plan and section.

(1) Entrance passage (dromos), 6 by 37 metres (20 by 121 feet), at the end of which was a polychrome portal with attached columns of the Cretan type (but with an Egyptian cavetto moulding below the abacus and echinus) supporting a lintel with Minoan motifs, from which the pressure of the upper masonry was deflected by a corbelled triangular tympanum; (2) the main offering chamber (tholos) with its corbel vault, 14.5 metres (47 feet 7 inches) in diameter and 13.2 metres (43 feet 4 inches) high, was once decorated with rows of metal rosettes; (3) burial chamber.

The subterranean tholos tomb, monumentalising the primitive Aryan circular hut, is the grandest of several tomb types, including rectangular pits lined and sealed with stone and rock-cut chambers. The earliest Mycenaean tholoi, built largely of rubble, date from the late 16th century BC; the latest, of dressed stone, from late in the 13th century BC. A precedent for them has been found in the early Minoan ossuaries common throughout Crete – though these were built above ground. Most later Cretans were buried in rock-cut rooms – though several of these imitated grand houses with rectangular rooms and flat roofs.

85 **Tiryns, citadel** c. 1400–1200 BC, plan.

(1) Entrance ramp, c. 1280; (2) passage crossed by gates; (3) first portico (propylaeum), entrance to forecourt; (4) second propylaeum, entrance to main court; (5) ruler's main reception room (megaron) with central hearth, vestibule and portico; (6) private court and megaron.

The entrance sequence, involving the exposure of the unprotected right flank of an approaching enemy and turns through repeated right angles, has early Anatolian precedents (for instance, at Alisar). The propylaea, at the head of the entrance passage, are regularly planned structures consisting of similar colonnaded porticos set back to back: the type clearly recalls the propylaeum at the foot of the ceremonial staircase at Knossos and is also related to the gates of the Trojans and Hittites. At 9.8 by 11.8 metres (32 feet by 38 feet 6 inches), the main megaron, with its four columns surrounding the king's hearth, was the grandest of the type. To its west was the royal bath and service rooms. In parallel to the east was a private court. An earlier ante-court and porchless megaron are entered through separate corridors from both propylaea.

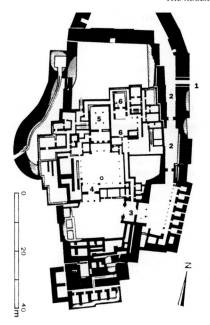

86 Tiryns, citadel, portico of main megaron
reconstruction.

The reconstruction assumes the pitched roof and gable, almost certainly wrongly. Like the rest of the palace but in contrast to the defence works, the main megaron was built c. 1200 BC of adobe and timber in the Cretan manner. The decorative motifs were Cretan too. The frieze with half roundels separated by verticals in triads (a common Cretan motif), reconstructed from surviving fragments of alabaster and glass, was probably a dado rather than a cornice moulding.

In the main court is an open altar, suggesting that like its Cretan predecessors the Achaean palace was a sacred complex. Apart from tombs and palaces, there is no specifically religious architecture of any importance dating from the Achaean age.

ment of the complex: the porticoed megaron where the king actually lived, its scale and order enhancing the dignity of its occupant. The formula is repeated on a smaller scale in parallel, as at Troy.

The triumph of reason

The formal planning and heroic fortifications of the Mycenaeans are in stark contrast with the organic growth and seeming lack of defences of the rampart-less Cretan seats of power (see 75, pages 176–77), though in both cases the irregular line of approach follows a universal principle of defensive planning – security depends on making entry as difficult as possible for an enemy, and certainly on denying them an axial line. Guided by pragmatism for security and by reason for hierarchy, the Mycenaeans overlaid the defensive on to the ceremonial, the baffling on to the ordered. For

87 **Tiryns, citadel, entrance passage and inner gate.**

Note the massive blocks of undressed masonry, with courses corbelled and inclined to form a triangular vault. Typical of the early Achaeans and their Aryan cousins in Anatolia but attributed by later ages to the giant race of Cyclopes, such megalithic masonry is called 'cyclopean'.

the Cretans, on the other hand, prestige was won in the service of security by mystifying design. The labyrinth is essential to the myth of the Minotaur which lurked at the heart of Minos' palace. But among the youths sent annually as tribute to Knossos, the Athenian prince Theseus was able to kill the monster and unravel the labyrinth with a string of twine given him by the Cretan king's daughter: reason triumphed over mysticism.

The disparate approaches adopted by the builders of Knossos and Tiryns – one arousing emotion, the other appealing to reason – are characteristic respectively of earth mother-worshipping people, baffled by the mystery of fecundity, and of sky-god worshippers, alert to the terror of divine wrath and striving to understand its purpose in analysis of the order of the cosmos. Given the complexity of early Aegean history, this may be seen as simplistic, but it enshrines an essential truth: that the male and female principles represented the attitudes of mind of pastoralists and agriculturalists respectively and that these attitudes of mind lie behind approaches to architecture – as we shall continue to see when we turn to the classical tradition of Greece (see volume 2, HELLENIC CLASSICISM).

After the disappearance of the Hittites, their type of order was sustained in a vacuum by various city-states to the south-east of Anatolia and north-west of Syria. The porticos of the palaces at Ugarit[88] and Alalakh[89] were screened like those of Hattusas – though with columns rather than piers on one side only – and flanked by two square chambers. At Alalakh one of these leads sideways into the court before the audience hall, but at Ugarit the portico leads straight to the hall and the court is beyond, to the right.

The bit-hilani

The columned portico, flanked by square chambers and leading to a rectangular reception room, is in essence the so-called bit-hilani, which distinguishes the remains of the formidable fortified citadels of the early 1st-millennium Syrian neo-Hittites and Urartians, their battered walls punctuated by towers. At Carchemish and Cinjirli,[90] the Syrian form incorporates square towers – like the Hittite city gate. At

88 OVERLEAF **Ugarit (Ras Shamra), palace** 13th century BC, view of the remains with bit-hilani portico in the foreground and the main court beyond.

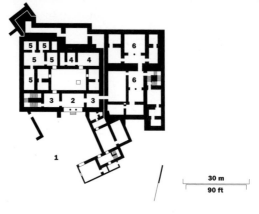

89 Alalakh (Tell Atchana), Palace of Niqmepa c. 1500 BC, plan.

(1) Entrance to the outer court; (2) vestibule with colonnaded portico and side chambers (3), anticipating the bit-hilani; (4) small apartment with bedroom and bathroom; (5) large apartment with antechamber, bedrooms and bathroom; (6) annexe with megarons.

The main rooms had a dado of orthostats rising to about a metre (3 feet 3 inches), like those of the nearby Palace of Yarimlim where the plan form is also anticipated.

30 m
90 ft

90 **Cinjirli, upper palace** 8th century BC, plan.
  (1) Court; (2) bit-hilani entrance to main apartment's
reception room, bedroom, bathroom and cubicles; (3) bit-
hilani entrance to self-contained apartment's bedroom and
bathroom; (4) detached bit-hilani block.

91 **Adilcevaz, Urartian relief** 7th century BC (Ankara, National Museum).

The relief shows the winged storm god Teiseba against defence walls typical of fortresses from time immemorial. Beyond the literal, the Urartian artist's extreme elongation of the tower buttresses suggests the representation of a great columned hall in elevation and section simultaneously

– especially since three-dimensional objects are viewed through them.

A regular succession of towers, providing cover for the recessed main face of the wall, is known from the mid 6th-millennium settlement at Hacilar in south-west Anatolia. Battering (thickening of the base against sappers and miners and for the bouncing of missiles), implied in the mound below the late 5th-millennium fortifications of Mersin in south-east Anatolia, was fully developed in the mid 3rd-millennium walls of Troy. Wall walks, high above the enemy, are rare survivals, but mid 2nd-millennium Hittite clay models show them projecting with crenellations for the protection of marksmen. These are characteristically stepped in Assyrian reliefs from the early 1st millennium – as, later, with the Babylonian Ishtar Gate and its context (see 18, pages 60–61). It is unclear from the reliefs whether the projection of the wall walk in corbelled masonry left holes (machicolation) through which missiles could be dropped on scalers or sappers, though the technique developed from the practice of ringing the tops of towers with timber hoardings. This was evidently widespread by the mid 2nd millennium.

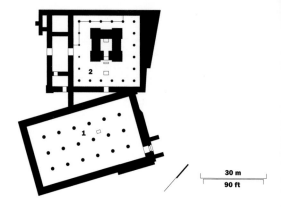

92 **Urartu (Altintepe), palace and/or temple**
7th century BC, plan.
  (1) Colonnaded hall entered from the east;
(2) shrine with bit-hilani entrance to the west.

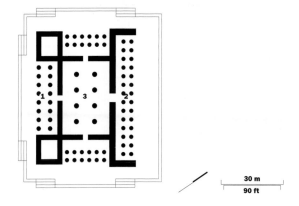

93 **Pasargadae (Persia), camp-palace of Cyrus
the Great, apadana** c. 540 BC, plan.
  Note the bit-hilani porticos (1) and loggia (2)
surrounding the colonnaded hall (3).

94 **Pasargadae, camp-palace of Cyrus the Great, apadana**.

Overlooked by a great platform built of cyclopean masonry, the three pavilions of Cyrus' palace were informally disposed like the tents of a camp in an enclosure. All had tent-like columned halls. The enclosure was entered through a portal guarded by winged, human-headed bulls related to the Assyrian Lamassu (see 67, page 162).

The columns of the apadana were 11 metres (36 feet) high, double those of its porticos. The bases of the main columns (in black stone in contrast with the white shafts) recall the Ionic torus. Little remains of the capitals, though

Urartu,[91–92] the colonnaded entrance screen was replaced by an arch but numerous columns were used to support the roof of the inner shrine-chamber and adjacent audience hall.

Sustaining a long tradition, the bit-hilani portico is clearly related to the porticos of Troy and Tiryns, the earliest built no later than the end of the 3rd millennium BC. On the other hand, syncretic works like the complex at Urartu also perpetuate the many-poled marquee and anticipate the great Achaemenid apadana (see volume 3, IMPERIAL FORM). From its first appearance in stone in the camp of Cyrus the Great at Pasargadae,[93–94] the apadana ceded little in monumentality to the festival halls of the pharaohs, and oriental potentates were never to forget it – or its origin in the tent.[95]

they appear to have anticipated later Achaemenid practice. The pavilion was partially screened: its ceremonial purpose was proclaimed in the reliefs of the king and symbolic animals on the jambs of the doors.

95 OVERLEAF **Indian miniature painting** ruler enthroned in campaign tent, early 19th century.

glossary

ABACUS flat slab forming the top of a CAPITAL.

AISLE side passage of a BASILICA or temple, running parallel to the NAVE and separated from it by COLUMNS or PIERS.

ANTA a PILASTER at the end of a side wall of, for instance, a temple, between two of which one or more COLUMNS may be placed, which are then IN ANTIS.

APADANA columned HYPOSTYLE HALL, usually square in plan, with a PORTICO on one or more sides. (See page 217.)

APSE semi-circular domed or vaulted space, especially at one end of a BASILICA.

ARCUATE shaped like an arch. Hence (of a building) arcuated, deploying arch structures (as opposed to TRABEATED). (See page 56.)

ASTRAGAL small moulding with circular or semi-circular cross-section.

AXIS line used to establish geometry around which a building is designed. Hence axial plan, in which the building is related to fundamental two- or three-dimensional base lines.

BASILICA temple or other public building, consisting principally of a COLONNADED rectangular space enclosed by an ambulatory or having a central NAVE and side AISLES, often with an APSE, and generally lit by a CLERESTORY.

BASTION structure projecting from the angle of a defensive wall, enabling enhanced vision and mobility for a garrison.

BATTERING reinforcement of wall bases by building a sloping supporting structure.

BEAM horizontal element in, for instance, a TRABEATED structure. (See page 65.)

BLIND WALL wall without doors or windows.

BIT-HILANI columned PORTICO, specifically of 1st millennium BC Syria. (See page 217.)

BUTTRESS support, usually stone, built against a wall to reinforce or take load.

CAPITAL top part of a COLUMN, supporting the ENTABLATURE.

CAVETTO style of concave moulding with a quarter-circular cross-section.

CIBORIUM canopy raised on columns so as to form a covering above an altar or tomb, for example.

CLERESTORY windowed upper level providing light for a double-storey interior.

COLONNADE line of regularly spaced COLUMNS.

COLUMN vertical member, usually circular in cross-section, functionally structural or ornamental or both, usually comprising a base, shaft and CAPITAL.

COLUMN IN ANTIS a COLUMN deployed in a PORTICO between ANTAE as opposed to standing proud of the façade.

CORBEL course of masonry or support bracket, usually stone, for a BEAM or other horizontal member. Hence corbelled: forming a stepped roof by deploying progressively overlapping corbels. (See pages 56, 200.)

CORNICE projecting moulding forming the top part of an ENTABLATURE. More generally, a horizontal ornamental moulding projecting at the top of a wall or other structure.

COVE/COVING curved concave moulding forming or covering the junction between wall and ceiling.

CYCLOPEAN MASONRY masonry made up of massive irregular blocks of undressed stone. (See page 206.)

DADO the middle part, between base and CORNICE, of a PEDESTAL, or the lower part of a wall when treated as a continuous pedestal.

DAIS raised platform, usually at one end of an internal space.

DROMOS entrance to a building, particularly a tomb, in the form of a long narrow passage often between COLONNADES.

ECHINUS quarter-round convex projection or moulding on a cushion supporting the ABACUS of the CAPITAL of a COLUMN.

ENTABLATURE part of the façade immediately above the COLUMNS, usually composed of a supportive architrave, decorative frieze and projecting CORNICE.

FILLET top part of a CORNICE, or generally a decorative moulding in the shape of a narrow raised band.

GLACIS slope or ramp in front of, for instance, a defensive wall.

HYPOSTYLE HALL hall with a roof supported by numerous COLUMNS,

LINTEL horizontal member over a
window or doorway, or bridging the
gap between two COLUMNS or PIERS.
(See page 196.)

MACHICOLATION gallery or parapet
projecting on CORBELS from the
outside of defensive walls, with holes
for missiles to be dropped or thrown.

MASTABA Egyptian mud-brick structure
built above tombs, a predecessor of
the pyramids. (See page 98.)

MEGARON rectangular hall forming the
principal interior space of a palace.

NAVE central body of principal interior
of, for instance, a BASILICA.

OBELISK tall monolith of more or less
square cross-section, tapering towards
the top and ending in an integral
pyramid. (See page 113.)

ORTHOSTATS stone slabs deployed
vertically to form the lower part of
a wall.

PEDESTAL base supporting a COLUMN
or statue.

PIER supporting pillar for wall or roof,
often of rectangular cross-section.

PILASTER a PIER of rectangular cross-
section, more or less integral with and
only slightly projecting from the wall
which it supports.

PLINTH rectangular base or base support
of a COLUMN or wall.

PORTICO entrance to a building featuring
a COLONNADE.

POST vertical element in, for instance,
a TRABEATED structure.

PROPYLAEUM gateway, especially to
a temple enclosure.

PYLON monumental tower, often
associated with a temple gateway.
(See page 67.)

RELIEF carving, typically of figures,
raised from a flat background by
cutting away more (high relief) or less
(low relief) of the material from which
they are carved. (See pages 48–49.)

REVETMENT decorative reinforced facing
for a retaining wall.

STELE upright stone marker, often
a tombstone, in the shape of a
COLUMN or panel, usually with
decorative carving and/or inscription.
(See page 24.)

THOLOS dome, either freestanding or
forming the centre of a circular
building. (See page 200.)

TORUS large convex moulding, typically at the base of a COLUMN, of more or less semi-circular cross-section.

TRABEATED structurally dependent on rectilinear POST and BEAM supports. (See page 65.)

TYMPANUM area, usually recessed, formed by a LINTEL below and an arch above. (See page 196.)

VOUSSOIR wedge-shaped stone deployed in building an arch. Hence voussoir arch, where such stones are used.

WATTLE AND DAUB method of making walls using thin twigs (wattles) interwoven and then plastered with mud or clay (daub).

ZIGGURAT building composed of a stepped series of concentric rectangles, the whole forming a truncated pyramidal structure. (See pages 72–73.)

The books listed below are those the author found particularly useful as sources of general information on the architecture covered in this volume.

Baines, J and Málek, J, *Atlas of Ancient Egypt*, Oxford 1980

Beek, M A, *Atlas of Mesopotamia*, London 1962

Collon, D, *Ancient Near Eastern Art*, London 1995

Cottrell, A, *The Minoan World*, London 1979

Curtis, J E, *Ancient Persia*, London 1989

Edwards, I E S, *The Pyramids of Egypt*, Harmondsworth 1947, revised edition 1961

Evans, A J, *The Palace of Minos at Knossos*, volumes I–VII, London 1921–36

Frankfort, H, *Art and Architecture of the Ancient Orient*, London 1954

Ghirshman, R, *Persia: from the origins to Alexander the Great*, London 1964

Graham, J W, *The Palaces of Crete*, Princeton 1962

Gurney, O R, *The Hittites*, revised edition, London 1990

Herzfeld, E, *Iran in the Ancient East*, Oxford 1941

Kuhrt, A, *The Ancient Near East c. 3000–300 B.C.*, 2 volumes, London and New York 1995

Lange, K and Hirmer, M, *Egypt: Architecture, Sculpture, and Painting in Three Thousand Years*, 4th edition, London 1968

Lloyd, S, *Early Anatolia*, Harmondsworth 1956

Lloyd, S, *Art of the Ancient Near East*, London 1961

Lloyd, S, *The Archaeology of Mesopotamia*, London 1978

Lloyd, S and Müller, H W, *Ancient Architecture*, London 1986

Macqueen, J G, *The Hittites*, London 1986
Smith, W S, *The Art and Architecture of Ancient Egypt*,
    London 1958
Upham Pope, A, ed., *A Survey of Persian Art from Prehistoric
    Times to the Present*, London and New York 1938

Sources of illustrations

pages 77, 80 E Strommenger and M Hirmer, *5000 Years of the Art
of Mesopotamia*, New York 1964; page 95 K Lange and M Hirmer,
*Egypt: Architecture, Sculpture, and Painting in Three Thousand
Years*; pages 102, 105, 115, 126, 127, 128, 143, 146, 159 Leonardo
Benovolo, *Storia della Città*, Rome 1975; page 114 A Badawy,
A History of Egyptian Architecture, Cairo 1964; page 152 E Bald-
win Smith, *Egyptian Architecture*, New York 1938; pages 200, 203
Hugh Plommer, *Ancient and Classical Architecture* (volume I of
Simpson's History of Architectural Development), London 1956;
page 204 W B Dinsmoor, *The Architecture of Ancient Greece*, re-
vised edition London 1950

index

Figures in bold refer to the text; those in ordinary type refer to captions; and those in ordinary type with an asterisk refer to illustrations.

map

Aegean
Sea

LYDI

Ionian Sea

IONIA

Mediterranean Sea

EARLY CIVILISATIONS